HOW TO BE A MENTALIST

HOW TO BE A
MENTALIST

MASTER THE SECRETS BEHIND THE HIT TV SHOW

SIMON WINTHROP

BERKLEY BOULEVARD BOOKS, NEW YORK

THE BERKLEY PUBLISHING GROUP
Published by the Penguin Group
Penguin Group (USA) Inc.
375 Hudson Street, New York, New York 10014, USA
Penguin Group (Canada), 90 Eglinton Avenue East, Suite 700, Toronto, Ontario M4P 2Y3, Canada
(a division of Pearson Penguin Canada Inc.)
Penguin Books Ltd., 80 Strand, London WC2R 0RL, England
Penguin Group Ireland, 25 St. Stephen's Green, Dublin 2, Ireland (a division of Penguin Books Ltd.)
Penguin Group (Australia), 250 Camberwell Road, Camberwell, Victoria 3124, Australia
(a division of Pearson Australia Group Pty. Ltd.)
Penguin Books India Pvt. Ltd., 11 Community Centre, Panchsheel Park, New Delhi—110 017, India
Penguin Group (NZ), 67 Apollo Drive, Rosedale, North Shore, 0632, New Zealand
(a division of Pearson New Zealand Ltd.)
Penguin Books (South Africa) (Pty.) Ltd., 24 Sturdee Avenue, Rosebank, Johannesburg 2196,
South Africa

Penguin Books Ltd., Registered Offices: 80 Strand, London WC2R 0RL, England

The publisher does not have any control over and does not assume any responsibility for author or
third-party websites or their content.

This book was not authorized, prepared, approved, licensed or endorsed by any entity involved in
creating or producing *The Mentalist* television series.

PRINTING HISTORY
Berkley Boulevard trade paperback edition / January 2011

Library of Congress Cataloging-in-Publication Data

Winthrop, Simon.
  How to be a mentalist : master the secrets behind the hit TV show / Simon Winthrop.—1st ed.
    p. cm.
  Includes bibliographical references.
  ISBN 978-0-425-23651-2
  1. Observation (Psychology)   2. Apperception.   3. Memory.   4. Deception.
5. Body language.   6. Hypnotism.   I. Title.
  BF323.O2W56 2011
  153.7—dc22

                                                                            2010030310

PRINTED IN THE UNITED STATES OF AMERICA

10 9 8 7 6 5 4 3 2 1

CONTENTS

Who Is This Person Called The Mentalist?

Who do you think knows you best? Your spouse, perhaps? Or maybe a parent or best friend?

But how well does that person really know you? For the most part, that person only knows what you've been willing to share with him or her, or what that individual has actually experienced with you. He or she has a limited, filtered viewpoint.

So imagine walking into a room and learning seconds later that you've been read. Someone standing across the room—someone you've never met—can tell you more about the *real* you than any of the people closest to you. This stranger can easily spout off your profession, your tax bracket, and what you ate for breakfast. He or she can pinpoint the areas of your life about which you feel most confident, and those where you struggle. This individual can shed light on some of your deepest, darkest secrets, and maybe even claim to communicate with one of your deceased relatives.

It's as if this person has known you your entire life. Or rather, it's as if this person has been watching you all of your life and has seen inside your head.

Who is this seemingly omniscient person?

A mentalist!

Mentalists have been around for centuries. One could argue that some of the first mentalists were actually the prophets and oracles of ancient times. Over the years, they took on the role of entertainer. Now you can find some of them at carnivals and fairs, reading the palms of those willing to plop down $5 or more. Others take the form of "faith healers" or psychics who say they can communicate with the dead or read your thoughts.

The most famous mentalist right now is Patrick Jane, featured in CBS's hit drama *The Mentalist*. Jane, a fictional character, uses his ability to read people in order to help the California Bureau of Investigation (CBI) solve heinous crimes.

Every episode begins with a definition of the term "mentalist": "Someone who uses mental acuity, hypnosis and/or suggestion. A master manipulator of thoughts and behavior." Patrick Jane demonstrates most or all of these abilities in every episode of the show. His unique practices often end up being more productive in catching criminals than forensic technology is or the CBI's other more conventional investigative methods.

In his past career Jane was a high-profile television personality who professed an ability to communicate with the dead. Then a vicious serial killer—enraged by what he perceived as Patrick's fraudulent claims of psychic ability—murdered the mentalist's wife and young daughter. Traumatized and remorseful, Patrick left the limelight, shed his more theatrical mystical identity, and started work as a full-time consultant with the police.

And so begins the classic yarn of a budding superhero using his powers for good. Except that these powers can be taught. You can be a mentalist just like Patrick Jane.

Mentalist vs. Magician

You may be wondering what the difference is between a mentalist and a magician. Well, mentalists and magicians are a lot alike. Many magicians are also mentalists, and vice versa. In both cases, individuals use secret methods and knowledge to create entertainment for an audience based on mystery. They differ in that the magician may claim to have magical powers, such as the ability to restore a cut rope or cause a particular card to rise to the top of the deck, while a mentalist bases his or her performances on more intellectual and knowledge-based abilities.

As I said, one of the most impressive of the mentalist's skills is the seeming ability to effortlessly and instantly observe a person and somehow know that person without their having ever previously met. This "instant observation" typically is useful when Patrick Jane finds himself dealing with suspects and witnesses who may be less than honest. And while you might want to learn Jane's tricks to deal with the liars in your life, the skills can also serve as an impressive icebreaker at the next holiday party you attend.

There's really no aspect of your life that wouldn't benefit from some mentalism. These techniques can prove useful in the boardroom, on the playing field, or when you're making a large purchase. Is the salesman pulling your leg or offering a sound deal?

We all crave more information. But can we ever know too much? That's an interesting question, and one I'll explore a bit more later in the book. Sometimes I've found that this gift can also become a burden.

Are Mentalists Psychic?

Some people believe that the skill of being able to read an object is actually a rather magical process. They call this "psychometry," or the ability to sense vibrations and energies from objects.

Psychometry is basically a form of so-called extrasensory perception (ESP). "Extrasensory perception" refers to the ability to gain information about a person or object through seemingly supernatural means. The term "psychometry" was coined by a physician, Joseph Rodes Buchanan, in the 1800s. He theorized that every object gives off an energy or emanation, and that from this we can receive messages about the object and its past or present owner.

Hogwash!

Let me say in no uncertain terms that Jane is not a psychic, nor does he benefit from extrasensory perception. Neither do I. In fact, Patrick Jane takes every opportunity to expose psychics as frauds. Having fooled audiences for years himself, he knows that even the most convincing mediums are really just showmen and con men. There is no energy coming from an object placed in your hand, at least not an energy that will tell you what the object's owner ate for lunch.

We have all had experiences where we knew or sensed something without understanding exactly how. Different people have different levels of sensitivity and awareness, such as acute hearing or a heightened sense of smell, and it's certainly possible that at such times we are simply more in tune with these perceptions.

But we're not operating within the realm of a comic book or an HBO series. This is real life. In real life we can uncover information about an object's owner by being perceptive and training ourselves to be skillful observers. Psychics claim to have gifts beyond those of the "normal" person; powers that may come and go based on the situation. And they use these so-called energies to guide their believers to make certain life decisions.

Mediums go one step further and claim to be able to communicate with the spirits of the departed. Their purpose is to use these abilities to guide others in making big choices, and they also describe their abilities as "gifts," rather than as a reliable skill set. In my experience, anyone can talk to ghosts, but I have yet to meet anyone who had a ghost talk back.

While not psychic, Jane is a modern-day Sherlock Holmes, using all the skills of an astute observer and taking them to brand-new heights. These are skills that any of us can learn and hone.

Who Am I?

You may wonder who I am, and why I feel I'm qualified to teach you how to become a mentalist.

Well, I myself am a magician and mentalist.

I've spent decades perfecting my craft and have uncovered secrets that you can't find in books, online, or in videos. I've been performing for years and have entertained many celebrities, including Bruce Willis, Demi Moore, Jack Nicholson, Tom Cruise, Arnold Schwarzenegger, and the Clintons.

But more importantly, I'm just like you. I have no special superpowers, and I don't have any so-called paranormal abilities. I sleep, eat, walk, and talk the same way you do. But I have harnessed my mentalist abilities. I guarantee that my senses are much more acute than yours. My memory is larger and more detailed. When I speak to people, I can read them in a way that you wouldn't be able to even if you'd known that person for years.

That's what makes me a mentalist, and that's why I am able to teach you how to become the same.

Elements of a Mentalist

In this book I'm going to share with you all of the basic elements you'll need to become a mentalist yourself. That's not to say you'll be taking over my act in Las Vegas overnight. Many of these skills take time, practice, and experience to hone. But once you've read all the basics, you'll be equipped to train yourself to improve on them and to understand better just how the mind works.

- *Think Smart, Not Hard*
  Patrick Jane makes it all look so easy, doesn't he? In this first chapter we'll explain how. In order to help your brain work best, I'll teach you how to reduce stress, sharpen your focus, and boost your mind power.

- *A Flawless Memory*
  So many of Patrick's abilities are based on what he remembers from previous experiences. He can apply that knowledge to a current situation and make certain deductions based on that. He has an uncanny ability to remember items from a crime scene or the faces from a specific location at a certain time. All of these skills come in handy with crime solving, and an incredible memory can also make for some impressive party tricks.

- *Observation Is Key*
  In the series pilot someone asks Patrick, "Are you psychic?" He answers, "No. Just paying attention." Indeed, Patrick Jane seems to notice things that most people would never see. He's trained his powers of observation so that nothing gets by him. Few people understand just how much you can learn by simply paying attention.

- *Lie Detection*
  Much of Patrick Jane's usefulness to the CBI is based on his abilities as a human lie detector. Often he'll sit in on an interrogation,

and after the questioning's finished, his partner, Teresa Lisbon, will pull him aside to see if the suspect was being truthful. I'll share with you some telltale signs for spotting a liar, and some surefire techniques for getting to the truth.

■ *Controlling Your Audience*

It's important that the mentalist always have the upper hand, whether it's in front of an auditorium full of people or in an interrogation room. I'll tell you how you can stay confident and keep everybody else off balance. So much of being powerful is based on appearances and perception.

■ *Hypnotism*

Going one step further with this power of control, I'll show you the basics of hypnosis and clear up just what is and isn't doable when you have someone in a trance. Patrick Jane often uses hypnosis—much to Lisbon's chagrin—to get witnesses and suspects to reveal information they usually wouldn't feel comfortable sharing. I'll show you how you can even perform self-hypnosis to help you accomplish things you may not otherwise achieve.

■ *Readings*

Few things can amaze an audience like a detailed, accurate cold reading. I'll show you how much you can learn about a person by simply observing that person and understanding certain things about the human condition. Patrick uses cold reads to throw off suspects and make them more likely to talk.

▪ *Tricks of the Trade*

I'll show you how you can put all of these tools together to pull off some amazing tricks to astonish your friends and family.

Armed with all of these skills, you'll be well on your way to becoming a mentalist as amazing and respected as Patrick Jane.

CHAPTER ONE

Thinking Smart, Not Hard

Most of us have been raised in a society that teaches us that the hardest worker wins the race, whatever that race may be. We work, work, work, and work some more, never giving ourselves time to think, and more important, never giving our brain time to rest.

When in days before we may have completed a "hard day's work," we now must attempt to complete a "smart day's work." At least that's how a mentalist looks at things.

The real secret to Patrick Jane's charisma, charm, and ability to think so fast lies in his ability to think smart, not necessarily outwork the room. This laid-back attitude isn't always popular with Jane's coworkers. They question whether he's taking his job seriously, but they can't argue with the kind of results he produces. Jane wouldn't be quite so effective at catching criminals if he were more concerned with working hard than with working smart.

In order to best use the skills we all have hidden inside of us, we must first look after our own minds, use them well and treat them as muscles. Most important, we must begin to love our minds and give them a great deal more respect.

Getting Rid of Stress

Anyone who's ever seen a cop in action knows that police are always sprinting toward dangerous situations that other people would run away from—and most crime fighters will tell you that they love the action. They say the "rush" makes them more efficient, more focused, able to better remember things. There may be some truth to this, as long as life on the edge doesn't cross the line into anxiety. Medical research shows that people who are anxious produce "stress hormones," such as cortisol, which damage brain cells.

We're all stressed all the time, aren't we?

It's the way the world works, the way our society works. We're stressed about getting the kids out the door and to school, and then we're stressed about work. And we spend our day stressed at work until we get home, where we're stressed about getting the kids to eat their dinner and get down for bed in time.

Then we're stressed as we lie in bed and think about doing it all again tomorrow.

So we spend our lives stressed, and unfortunately most of us have come to accept living that way. But there are several reasons why we shouldn't accept it. For the purpose of this book, it's important to realize that stress clouds our ability to see the things we need to see as we try to achieve mentalist status, which is, of course, our goal.

In this chapter I will teach you some simple ways to reduce your stress levels. It has been proven repeatedly that when we are stressed we tend to make bad decisions, and in learning to reduce stress we begin to think smart and not hard.

But there's another very important reason we should calm down, think smart, and avoid stress: our health. It's not healthy to be stressed all the time. There is a direct correlation between our stress and anxiety and our physical well-being. So why not cut the stress out of your life right now?

CUT THE STRESS, FEEL BETTER

Don't believe me that stress can impact your health? There are hundreds if not thousands of studies out there that will without question tell you that stress contributes to the decline of physical health. You're probably already aware of all the ways stress can affect your heart: It increases blood pressure and can result in abnormal heart rhythms. Your worries can also manifest themselves as headaches, ulcers, and skin conditions. But it doesn't end there . . .

High levels of stress can be contributing factors in cancer and fibromyalgia. They can also weaken your immune system's ability to fight off colds and other infections.

Those are only some of the worst-case scenarios. At best,

stress will keep you from sleeping, and in your unrest you'll be unable to think at your highest potential.

In order to work some mentalist magic, you need to be in good health: mentally and physically.

CUT THE STRESS, THINK CLEARER

You're reading this book because you want to be a mentalist. You want to be able to read items and people. You want to be able to discern what others are thinking. Well how do you expect to be able to read the thoughts of others if your own thoughts are clouded by stress?

Yes, stress can make us think differently than we would otherwise. I used the term "clouded," and that's exactly what it is. The cloud of stress can make us paranoid and negative, and can simply sway us in a direction that we wouldn't otherwise go.

If you're under a lot of pressure, your thoughts are starting out from a base of fear, anxiety, and negativity, and in turn your actions will originate from those feelings. Those unbalanced, negative emotions are not the calling card of a true mentalist, and so we must release and be free of them before we can achieve our goals.

Our first step to reducing our stress levels and clearing our minds of negativity is learning how to relax and enjoy the moment. You can't just go there cold turkey. After a life of stress, you can't simply say, "OK, I'm gonna stop and relax now." It's almost like alcoholism; we're addicted to the stress.

So for now let me be your sponsor who will get you out of this stress cloud. And let me show you the tool we'll use to get there: meditation.

Elements of Meditation

Meditation has many different uses that can benefit you and can be applied in practically every aspect of your life. First and foremost, the meditations I will go over can be used as tools to focus your mind with razorlike precision. You will be learning how to relax, yet at the same time fine-tuning your concentration and alertness.

I once spent a month in one of the most beautiful places in the world, Bangalore, India. Every morning during that month I would wake up in a serene location, and a few times a day I would take different meditation and yoga classes. I met great spiritual and healthy people, and I learned about the power of sitting in silence.

Believe it or not, I was silent for three days. I said nothing and heard no other voices for that entire time. It is an unbelievable exercise that helps you develop your intuitive abilities exponentially. With the silence inside, you recognize that words are not all they are cracked up to be. You get to really develop your mentalist abilities by releasing yourself from as many of your attachments as possible.

When you meditate, you want to absorb the energy that fills you. This absorption is also sometimes known as surrendering to the flow. As your muscles relax, your mind will quiet down and your intuition will become more aware.

Scientists and researchers have discovered many wonderful benefits from meditation, including:

Slowing down the aging process

Relief of pain

Increased energy levels

Lowering cholesterol

Reducing bacteria in the body

Increased blood flow to the brain, which enhances our thinking and improves our memory

So let's learn to meditate!

POSTURE

The first step toward proper and effective meditation is good posture. It's also best to find a quiet place that will be conducive to relaxation, where you won't be bothered by any outside distractions.

You do not have to have your spine perfectly straight and stiff like an ironing board, but to ensure a proper flow of energy you do not want a hunched back either. While positioning yourself, imagine that your body is situated like a spout waiting for the release of a spring of water. Sometimes the spring is subtle and just dribbles out, and sometimes it shoots out hard and forcefully from the top of your head. Obviously, nothing physical will be shooting from the top of your head, but a kind of release and energy will be, when this is done correctly, and you want to make sure your posture is erect, not kinked, to optimize that flow.

Or if that visual isn't helpful, you may want to imagine a silver cord attached at the very crown of your head and being pulled straight up into the heavens. With one end of this cord attached to you, the other end is attached in the stars, keeping you standing or sitting tall and rigid—but not uncomfortably.

BREATHING

There are several breathing exercises that I've found tremendously beneficial for balancing my energy. When someone tells you to "take a deep breath" when you're feeling overwhelmed, they're not giving you empty advice. Breathing can be very therapeutic, especially when used along with other relaxation techniques.

First let's talk about how breathing is important to not only meditation but how you live your everyday life. You can draw a direct correlation between the way you breathe and the way you feel. As I like to say, breathing is sort of like the timing belt for your body. If your timing belt doesn't run right, your car sputters and isn't efficient. But if your timing belt is working properly, your car should run smoothly.

My meditation mentor, Sri Sri Ravi Shankar, uses an amazing exercise called the "breath of fire" release. It's always best to have someone to instruct you with these techniques, especially if you're trying them for the first time. But these are the steps you will take during the exercise:

- First you'll start to take long, deep breaths naturally and comfortably. You'll be sitting cross-legged or on your knees with your hands palms up on the tops of your knees.

- You'll continue taking slow, long, deep breaths and start to focus on controlling the breathing from your diaphragm, instead of your upper chest and lungs.

- You'll feel your diaphragm contract and expand like a muscle—the secret is to concentrate on this movement.

- Now each time you exhale, you'll press the air out more forcefully, and when inhaling you'll suck it in deeper and stronger. This is known as an energized cleansing, and it feels *great*.

- You'll continue to suck in air and pump it out—in and out and up and down—faster and faster and faster, as if a snowball were barreling down a mountain and picking up speed. This will likely make you dizzy, so it's important to consult your doctor or health professional before attempting the exercise.

- After a period of time—probably about five minutes for beginners—you'll have reached a feverish pitch and won't be able to continue. At this point, you'll start slowing down and your breaths will become long and deep again for another five minutes.

I think you'll be amazed with how clear and focused you feel after performing this technique. But it's not the only breathing exercise that's helped me. You may find you have even better results with one of these other methods. Next I'm going to share a bit about a technique I learned during my travels in India: the healing breath.

Through the use of the healing breath, you should be able to let all of your outside distractions fall away.

There are a lot of Web sites and texts that refer to the healing breath and its associated spirituality. Some say you should look for a light or consider how much the universe loves you while you're breathing. But what we're going for here is to understand how you breathe and how that can calm your mind and body.

The best way to describe the healing breath is to first describe what it's not. Think about riding a bike behind another rider and watching the way the rider in front pedals his or her feet. If you can imagine it, the pedaling probably looks like the person stops, even for just a split second, at the top and bottom of the cycle. Now imagine looking at the same pedaling motion from the side. Does the motion ever truly stop or is it a continuous loop?

You'll find that it's a loop, and that's how your breathing during the healing breath should be. This continuous motion of breathing requires concentration and patience. You have to train your mind and your body to sit there and keep track of the breathing process. But the more you do it, the more you'll find that you are able to adapt it to activities other than simply sitting and thinking. The consistency that comes with the healing breath will bring harmony to your body and your mind. You will feel centered and have a much stronger awareness of your surroundings.

Finally, there's another amazing bit of breath work that can enhance your brain wave activities. The method I'm referring to is Holotropic Breathwork. It was invented by Christina Grof and Stanislav Grof, who was formerly chief of psychiatric research at the Maryland Psychiatric Research Center and assistant professor of psychiatry at Johns Hopkins University School of Medicine.

Holotropic breathing may seem rather unconventional if you've never experienced it before, but nevertheless, it can be very effective. The exercises are quite intense, so you must make sure you are in healthy physical shape and have a doctor approve your participation. It's also important to find a qualified certified practitioner to guide you through the experience.

This is not something you should try at home on your own, but I can tell you a little about what you can expect from a session. You enter a dimly lit room and are handed a blanket, a pillow, and a bottle of water. You lie on the floor, and an instructor guides you through a series of breathing exercises for thirty to forty minutes. The exercises are similar in depth and rapidity to hyperventilating. As you listen to powerful, climactic music, which moves your energies, you will fold into a fetal position, experiencing amazing psychic and visual projections. You'll also have a tremendous feeling of release.

Holotropic Breathwork has been known to relieve physical and emotional pain, assist with memory recall, increase self-awareness, and expand the mind both intuitively and creatively.

ATTITUDE

Keeping an open mind is essential to effective meditation. If you want to be able to achieve your meditation goals, you have to stop fueling your negativity. Not everyone is bad, and the illusion that you're the only right one and that you have to be in control all of the time will cause your brain to become resistant.

You will find a constant challenge lingering between your heart and mind. Your heart will want to continue on with the meditation while your mind will not. Your mind will want to stop early and move on to another task. But it is important that you resist this temptation as much as possible. As a beginner, you will notice your thoughts wandering. Keep returning your attention to the meditation, and surrender, as best as you can, to your objectives and focus this feeling and desire toward your heart and emotions.

Let's Meditate

When you start to introduce meditation into your life, you should plan on a ten-minute session every morning before eating. Gradually your sessions will increase and last for up to twenty minutes. This meditation will tend to keep you awake longer, so if you decide to do it in the evening then please do it before your evening meal.

Now that you have decided to meditate, choose a comfortable chair which allows you to sit upright. Loosen any tight clothing. If you are feeling extra tense, you can lean your head backward for a little self-massage by rolling your neck first left then right, then around in a circle to your left and around in a circle to your right, and stretching.

Now follow these steps:

1. Close your eyes. Inhale a deep breath to the count of five and then hold your breath for a count of four. Then slowly exhale to the count of eight. Repeat this ten times. Remember the healing breath exercise I discussed earlier. You never want to feel yourself coming to a complete stop in your breathing. Instead think of yourself as the pedal on a bike, continuing in a constant circular motion.

2. You can now relax with your normal breathing.

3. Focus your attention up to the third-eye area (the point between your eyebrows, on your forehead).

4. Don't let your chin droop. It should be tilted slightly upward. Allow your hands to rest easily on your lap, palms turned upward, which will allow you to be more open and receptive.

5. Make sure your spine and head are positioned upward and you have your legs either cross-legged or in a kneeling position.

6. Your mantra is the word "om." In your mind I want you to begin to repeat "om," but nothing needs to be heard, so just say it to yourself mentally.

7. Continue mentally repeating your mantra "om—om—om—om—om," and if other thoughts begin to distract you, just let

them dissolve. As mentioned earlier, meditation takes prac-tice, and it will be difficult at first not to let other thoughts pop into your head. You simply need to let these other thoughts disappear, without placing special attention on the dissolving process. Don't stress about it!

The meditation is intended to focus and relax you, enhancing your receptivity for awareness and intuition. Within two weeks of daily practice, you will notice a lot of changes. Your mind will become clearer and you will feel less stress. Your body might feel stronger and you'll likely have more energy. You'll also feel like you're more receptive to the world around you, observing more, with a feeling that all of your senses have been enhanced.

The Mind-Body Connection

EAT WELL

It shouldn't be surprising that your diet affects how your brain performs. It is often said that your brain is probably the greedi-est organ in your body, and it requires a very specific type of nutrition. As we grow older, the brain has less capacity to defend itself from daily threats like free radicals, inflammation, and oxidation. As brain cells age, they sometimes stop communi-cating with one another, slowing down essential processes like thinking, short-term memory retrieval, and the regeneration of new cells. A diet rich in antioxidants helps to maintain not only good health, but a smarter brain as well. Good sources of antioxidants are:

- *Vitamin A and beta-carotene:* carrots, spinach, cantaloupe, winter squash

- *Vitamin C:* citrus fruits, broccoli, and strawberries

- *Vitamin E:* nuts, seeds, vegetable oil, and wheat

But antioxidants aren't the only consideration for a better brain diet. Here are some other interesting connections between your mind and the things you put into your body:

- Scientific research also indicates that eating fish can indeed sharpen your memory. Most fish fat contains the polyunsaturated fatty acid DHA, which plays a significant part in the brain development of young children. Tests show that kids who consume foods containing adequate amounts of DHA score better on IQ tests than their peers. Fish also contains omega-3 fatty acids, which open up new communication centers in the brain's neurons.

- You'll note that Patrick Jane is not a smoker. That could be because of another finding suggesting that smoking can affect the ability of the brain to properly process information. Chain smokers have higher risks of impairing their visual and verbal memories. So the next time you think of smoking, remember that not only is it dangerous to your health, but you are sacrificing your memory functions as well.

■ Although investigators are notorious coffee fiends, caffeine (and alcohol) can cause anxiety and nervousness, which may prevent information from properly entering your mind. Memory works best when you are relaxed and focused.

■ ■

MAKE A MENTALIST NOTE

Poor memory is often a result of poor self-image. After all, memory starts and ends in the mind. So to have a healthy mind, believe that you can achieve anything you desire. Boost your self-esteem and be confident in your abilities—your attitude should be supportive of your goals. Meditating with a positive chant—something like "I can do whatever I set my mind to"—can help in this regard.

■ ■

EXERCISE REGULARLY

Another stress reducer: cardiovascular exercise, which improves blood circulation and is good for the heart and brain. Research indicates that walking helps release hormones that aid in regenerating new brain cells. If you're bored with just plain walking, engage in a sport that you love—basketball, volleyball, tennis, anything that excites you.

Exercising also lowers your risk of developing high blood

pressure, which can contribute to memory loss. So get up and get moving. Not only will you be getting a fit and healthy body, but you'll also sharpen your mind and improve your creativity (not to mention the fun and camaraderie you can have with your teammates and competitors).

A sound body is a great start, but you also need to specifically exercise your brain so that it doesn't deteriorate. Engage in games that will help you think. Talk to people, read informational books, listen to educational tapes, and make it a habit to continuously learn and experience new things. Remember that when your neurons die, they don't come back. You better use them, or you'll lose them.

MIND MUSIC

Elderly people suffering from dementia are said to have better reasoning about their personal history when there is music playing in the clinical area, as opposed to when they are questioned in silence, according to an experiment conducted by Elizabeth Valentine, a psychologist at the University of London and coauthor of new research on music and memory.

Increasingly, music is accompanying traditional medical therapies to help people heal faster. Experts say music has the power to calm and to energize the spirit.

British researchers conducted a test on twenty-three people (ages sixty-eight to ninety) with mild dementia. The test was done with different sounds playing in the background. While asking the questions, the researchers either played a familiar tune ("Winter," from Vivaldi's *Four Seasons*), novel music ("Hook," by Graham Fitkin), or prerecorded cafeteria noise—or they asked the questions in stillness. Over four weeks, each person was tested in all four situations.

The participants answered more questions correctly with sound in the background rather than silence, and they scored even better when music was playing.

"Whether the music was familiar or new did not seem to matter. The music probably aroused the participants and helped them focus," the researchers said.

LEARNING AND EMOTIONS

Your mood plays a vital role in perceiving, receiving, and retrieving information. More and more, we're seeing holistic approaches used to produce positive outlook and relaxation in clients and patients around the country. The mind-body balance definitely affects the way your mind works and the accessibility of its stored information. The goal is to make each situation as pleasant as possible—then your chances of recall are improved significantly.

Let's say you're studying for a test and you're feeling anxious over it. Normally, this would not be a pleasant way to spend your afternoon or evening, right? And the less pleasant the experience, the better the chance that your memory will try to shut it out as much as possible. So let's turn this around and make this a more soothing experience. Close your eyes and recall a picture, scenario, or relevant experience. A biology student might visualize the dissection lab that went perfectly, for example. A basketball player might picture the perfect shot. If you can link a relaxing past experience to the present, you'll start to feel more at ease and your memory will soak up the information at hand.

You can also do this by repeating a very positive statement, like "I'm a worthwhile person!" Remembering such words can boost confidence during exams or in periods of learning or even in more routine daily struggles. For example, let's say that your boyfriend has just broken up with you and you are devastated. Now you have to give a presentation in a meeting, which is bound to go badly, since you're just not focused at all. While picturing your boyfriend's face, say, "No matter what you say or do to me, I'm still a worthwhile person!" This puts you into a positive consciousness, relieves you from the stress of the situation, and helps to put your mental energy where it belongs—on the task before you.

There are also ways you can improve your mood by making changes in the space where learning takes place. Scented candles, aromatic objects, and the creation of the illusion of relaxation (with the use of verdant or calming colors such as pastels, earth tones, or non-solid shades) are some of the practical ways you can help yourself to relax while acquiring knowledge or information. In uncontrolled environments that require spontaneous reaction, simply re-create these vibes with mental pictures (imagine the blueness and calm of the sea, or the very refreshing scene of a green countryside).

The Power of the Mind

Now that it's primed, your mind can give you what you want, but you cannot be ridiculous in your requests. There is nothing mystical here, and I am not promising you that you can use your meditation practice as an ATM. While some books will teach you that simply focusing your mind on money will bring it, I make no such promises.

I do, however, believe that if you set a goal, focus on that goal, and keep it at the forefront of your attention, your mind can do incredible things to help you achieve it. Simply meditating daily over wanting $1 million won't bring it into your hands, especially if you don't have a plan. I suppose if you meditate on your plan to rob a bank, that could be one way, but I'm certainly not advocating it.

Seriously, though, you can set a goal in your mind of happiness, success, health, or any number of other things, and your mind can help you achieve those goals. I'll show you how.

FOLLOW A PLAN

What is it that you want, that you're trying to achieve? Whatever it is, you have to be specific and write it down. Deciding that you want to lose weight is too ambiguous. Be precise and laserlike in your desire. How much weight do you want to lose? What time frame do you have in mind?

Once you've written down your goal, the second step is

dedicating ten to fifteen minutes a day to meditating on that goal and committing yourself to whatever amount of time is required to achieve your goal. Can you make that promise to yourself?

Next you'll need to determine what that time frame for achieving your goal will be. It's important that this deadline you've set be reasonable. Is it realisitc to expect to lose fifty pounds in a week? Not even close. So don't just wing it when you're deciding on the timing. Put some thought into it.

The final step in your plan of action is identifying how you'll know when you've achieved your goal. Sometimes recognizing your success will be simple. For instance, the needle of your scale will indicate whether or not you've achieved your weight-loss goal. But what if your goal is based on an emotional or spiritual desire? How will you know when you've succeeded? How will you have been changed, and will you be able to identify that change?

Remember to make sure to put your goal in writing. Read it aloud daily, and also silently in your mind.

POSITIVE THINKING

You cannot underestimate the power of positive thinking. Before you even begin to meditate or take on any of the other steps that I'm about to lay out for you, I want you to simply sit and see yourself succeeding at whatever your goal is. What do the steps toward success look like, and what does achieving that ultimate goal look like?

Can you see yourself running the race? Can you see yourself winning?

You may be thinking that this all sounds cheesy and goofy, but it truly works. Even the most successful professional athletes will tell you that in the minutes and hours leading up to a game, match, or fight, they'll run through the upcoming competition in their minds. They'll see themselves shooting the basketball, swinging at a fastball, or throwing a kick or punch. This positive visualization gives them the confidence to succeed, but it also trains their subconscious. If your logical side sees something happening in your mind's eye, then your emotional side will believe it can happen, and that will give you a greater chance at success.

So go ahead and do that now. Sit and visualize your success. You're not simply daydreaming. You're playing the events out in your mind. It should almost feel real. Can you feel it?

Meditating on Your Goal

Now we're going to use those meditation skills I described and pair them with your visualization technique.

To begin, re-read your written goal and then follow all of the meditation and breathing steps we already went through. Except this time you'll end by visualizing your plan in your mind's eye. Visualize yourself on a large movie screen actually acting out all of the steps in your master plan and achieving your goal. This process of visualization could take a few seconds or several minutes. It's up to you, but try not to rush yourself.

You want to make sure you're being very descriptive in what

you're visualizing. What colors do you see? What do you smell? How do you feel when you achieve a certain step toward your goal? Do your best to experience all of these sensations.

Over time this exercise will start to feel more and more real. For the first couple of days or the first week you may keep those images in your mind on a movie screen. Eventually it will be as if you've moved them from the screen to a theater stage. From there, after a few days, I want the images to be in the same room with you. Imagine that it's all being acted out right in front of you. I want you to keep bringing it closer and closer, paying sharp attention to each happening.

Practice your visualization every day. The results can be powerful and amazing. The more you do this visualization, the closer it will come to being a reality.

WORKING OUT THE KINKS

The process I just described will come easier to some people than others. If you feel like you're struggling or just don't get it, I don't want you to lose hope. Remember, this is about relieving stress, not creating it.

Some people simply have a hard time creating pictures in their mind. You may be less of a visual person and operate more based on audible or emotional sensations.

If you've hit a stumbling block, close your eyes and do the following:

- Focus your imagination and clearly see a ruler. Visualize its sharp edge and firm features.

- Focus your imagination and clearly see a fruit. Imagine what it tastes like.

- Focus your imagination and clearly see a glass. Visualize the glass levitating off the table.

- Focus your imagination and clearly see green grass. Visualize the feeling of the wet grass between your toes.

- Focus your imagination and clearly see the moon. Imagine the way it would feel to be on it and in its atmosphere.

- Focus your imagination and clearly see a celebrity. Visualize being right next to that person. How does it feel?

- Focus your imagination and clearly see a candle. Visualize your hand waving across it.

- Focus your imagination and clearly see the sun. Imagine the feeling of you basking in its warmth.

If you find it easy to imagine any of the above, you can visualize anything and everything that you need to. These are just some exercises to get you there. Believe you can do it and you will.

By doing a mantra every morning and the visualization every night, you will put yourself on the way to a Patrick Jane–like focus and intuition.

MAINTAINING FOCUS

Now that you know your master plan and are growing closer to achieving it, you need to keep your eyes on the prize and make sure outside distractions don't get in the way. Avoid negativity and naysayers. You'll find that there are a lot of people out there who will try to bring you down. Make an effort to surround yourself with more positive influences. Does your partner or friend make you a better person?

More than anyone else, however, *you* must believe in yourself. Sure, we all have our ups and downs, times when our confidence gets shaken. It would be great to have a crystal ball to look into our future and know when we're making bad decisions and throwing ourselves off course. Given the recent economic tumult, we can't help but think how great it would be to have the ability to predict the stock market and know the best times to buy or sell. But that's just not the way life works. In the real world, we can see our finances plummet with one bad day on the NASDAQ. But as our world swings one way or the other, we can take control of how we react to it.

About ten years ago, I was invited to perform for a party at the home of Arnold Schwarzenegger. I ended up entertaining there on several occasions, and during one of these events, I found myself taking a walk around the grounds with the future governor of California. I made small talk and asked him how he was doing.

"I'm *always* fantastic," he said.

Like a dummy, I challenged him and said "You couldn't be. How could you *always* be fantastic?"

He gave it to me straight. "Who are you to tell me I'm not always fantastic? What's not fantastic? I have a beautiful home, beautiful wife, a great family, and I just finished another movie."

I said (a bit more humbly), "But don't you ever get in bad moods? *Those* aren't fantastic!"

He assured me he did. "We all do. But you come out of them . . . sometimes sooner than later. What you need to understand about moods is that they're all chemical and that a bad mood will pass and soon you'll be feeling good again."

I found what he said so powerful, and it really resonated with me. I thanked him for the insight. Clearly Arnold had learned to train his mind to stay positive and focused, just as he'd trained his body to be strong and healthy.

Applying what I've taught you about meditation, breathing, and visualization will help you train your own mind to navigate the ups and downs in your life. Even if you're not focused on a specific goal, at the very least you'll feel the stress drain from you, and the clouds of negativity will lift. As a result, you'll think more clearly and effectively.

Even as a mentalist, I experience highs and lows. On some nights I can feel the energy of the room more than on others. Generally, though, my performances are stronger, and my readings are more on target, when I've taken the time to meditate and focus. As they say, "Luck favors the well prepared."

And now, my friends, *you* are more prepared to put the rest of your mentalist skill set to use.

CHAPTER TWO

A Flawless Memory:
The Mentalist's Foundation

It's clear from watching Patrick Jane on *The Mentalist* that he has certain tools that make him a valuable consultant to the CBI. He quickly separates the truth from lies, he's an impeccable judge of character, and he has an uncanny ability to make keen observations that lead to accurate deductions. However, one thing serves as the lynchpin to all of the Mentalist's skills:

Memory.

You might think, "I don't have the kind of memory that Patrick Jane has—I can't do what he does!" Of course you can! If you remember nothing else, remember this: No one is born with a bad memory. Unless it's been physically damaged in some way, you can sharpen your memory with the proper knowledge and practice.

If you're not a crime fighter, why would you want to improve your memory? Well, for any number of reasons. In today's fast-paced, information-driven society, your memory of faces, names, facts, information, dates, events, and circumstances can mean the difference between success and failure. With a good memory, you don't have to fear misplacing essential items, plus you can overcome mental barriers that hinder you from achieving success in your career and personal life.

The Mentalist has a remarkable ability to walk into a room, recognize and link connections from the past to the present, and instantly process information about people and objects. Others see him as a freak of nature or a connection to the spirit world; in truth, he has simply honed his powers of recall.

MENTALIST SECRET

The first of the "big secrets" to becoming a real-life mentalist: Use your mind in ways that allow you to boost your confidence in the decisions you make. Patrick Jane is confident of his own conclusions and observations because he uses his mind in a manner that allows him to be 100 percent sure about his memories. With solid and accurate memories backing up his observations, there is no need for ifs, ands, or buts. Simple, confident, and clear thinking is the key.

Breaking It Down

A person's memory is composed of complicated neural connections in the brain. These connections are believed to be capable of holding millions of pieces of data. The capacity of your mind to retain past experiences in a highly organized manner gives you the ability to learn and create different new ideas.

Memory operates by the loading of images, sounds, tastes, smells, and sensations (touch) in a very organized and meaningful combination in your brain. There are three types of memory:

▪ Sensory memory is where temporary information is briefly recorded. When you walk along a busy street, for example, your sense of hearing is inundated with all kinds of noises. When you reach your destination, it's very unlikely that you'll be able to recall every single sound you heard, unless it somehow made an impression on your memory—hearing a scream or a gunshot, for example, would probably stand out as something worth noting.

▪ Short-term memory, characterized by twenty to thirty seconds of retention, involves a limited amount of information. Witnesses to crimes are usually reporting what they recall from their short-term memory, which by its very nature is short-lived and therefore a bit unreliable.

▪ Long-term memory involves consolidation of information for future reference. This is why you can remember things like your birthday, and also the reason you can build on what you've already learned. A well-developed sense of long-term memory also comes in handy for investigators like Patrick Jane, who rely on past experiences with other suspects and situations in order to crack the cases they're dealing with at the present time.

The human capability to process information is somewhat limited; therefore, not every stimulus is saved for later recall. There are plenty of things you don't remember from yesterday, last week, last month, or last year. That's the result of what we call *poor attention*. One of the most common causes of poor attention is simply a lack of interest.

On the other hand, people can have a very poor memory for many things, but be sometimes able to remember intricate details of certain situations, conversations, and so on. That's because they are interested in what they are observing. This is called *involuntary attention* and does not require special effort because it's based on our own interests, curiosities, or desires. Maybe you know someone who can recite baseball stats for an hour but can't remember to take his briefcase to work. That's because he's interested in sports and perhaps not so interested in his job.

This person would do well to train himself in the other type of attention, called *voluntary attention*, which is used to deal with objects, topics, people, and so on, that we don't necessarily find interesting. This requires effort, but it's the reason that a person who has no natural interest in medicine or science, for example, can still go on to become a successful doctor. That person simply throws all of his or her effort into learning the subject matter.

While every person has involuntary attention, only a few possess a developed sense of voluntary attention (and many of these folks are expert investigators like Patrick Jane, able to observe, process, and mentally file away the tiniest details about people, places, and things). While it's fine to go through life relying on involuntary attention, a finely honed sense of voluntary attention can open up many new doors. It can help you to impress your boss, become a great conversationalist, and keep much better track of your money. Patrick Jane uses voluntary attention to get to the bottom of the most heinous crimes, but you can use it simply to improve your daily life.

To sharpen your attention, you have to diligently practice the art of voluntary attention. Here are some successful strategies to help you get started:

- *Practice.* Focus on one object, person, or situation you find utterly uninteresting and study every detail about it until you are able to describe it. Pick a flower. Touch it. Smell it. Feel its texture. How many petals does it have? How long is the stem? What is the color and shape of the petals? Start to take notice of the details in the things around you: the places you visit, the people passing by, etc. You'll be surprised at the little things that you'll start to notice.

- *Eliminate distractions.* Even though you may have heard of multitasking, it is very difficult for people to truly focus on more than one thing at a time. For example, let's say you're a law student studying for the bar exam. You won't be able to truly absorb the information at hand if the radio is blaring, or if you're listening to your friends chitchatting in the next room. So when you're attempting to impress a memory onto your mind, eliminate as many distractions as you possibly can.

■ *Focus.* You're preparing for an important presentation at work tomorrow and a new employee is introduced to you. Although you know you were told her name, afterward you don't have the slightest idea what it is. Because you were concentrating on something that's far more important to you at the moment, the new person's name didn't make the cut in your memory— it was viewed as frivolous material. This is the kind of thing that can make you look aloof if it becomes a habit. On the other hand, someone who never forgets a name always makes a good impression. So if you want to remember something well, whether it's a name, a house number, or a specific date on the calendar, you have to intentionally shift your focus to that one thing and willfully commit it to memory.

■ *Give yourself a wake-up call.* It happens to everyone: You're physically working on a task, but your mind is somewhere else. Whenever you become aware that your thoughts are slipping, yell the word "stop!" in your mind. This will bring your drifting to a halt and redirect your attention. Remember that good concentration breeds good memory.

▪ *Get interested.* To develop good memorization skills, it helps if you like what you are doing. Try to put some heart into every activity; otherwise, there's slim chance you'll remember many aspects of it. As Leonardo Da Vinci said: "Just as eating against one's will is injurious to health, so study without a liking for it spoils the memory, and it retains nothing it takes in."

▪ *Make a mental note.* Just the act of stopping what you're doing to focus on a thought or impression is enough to embed it in your memory. Reminding yourself that you'll need the info later takes it to another level, making it something of an urgent matter. The next time you need to remember something like an appointment or a phone number, take a moment to commit it to memory and then say to yourself: "Take note of this!" You'll be astounded by what the subconscious can do for you.

▪ ▪

MENTALIST MEMORY EXERCISE
Taking Notice

To improve your recall of even the most minute details, try engaging in a mental review of each day's events. This can help you engage your attention during the day so that your recall of events is sharper, clearer, and available anytime for future retrieval.

Try to do this work in the evening, when you feel at ease, but don't do it after you retire. (The bed is made for sleeping, not for thinking!) Sit down alone at night and spend fifteen quiet, distraction-free minutes focusing on the important happenings of the day. After a few days, you will find that you can recall more and more. Events will come back to you more precisely and more clearly each time.

When you first begin this exercise, you may find that you have trouble recalling what you had for breakfast or what the cashier at the coffee shop looked like. But as your subconscious gets used to being called into duty, you'll find that you'll start to "take notice" of what happens *as* it happens, a skill that investigators across the country and around the world rely on heavily.

■ ■

SHARPENING YOUR SKILLS

Now that we've covered the basics of how your brain stores information, let's talk about how memories get "lost" in the dark, deep recesses of your mind and how you can get them back.

Contrary to popular belief, being *smart* is not synonymous with having a good memory or good retention—these things are really only a matter of knowing how your mind works and making the most of it. Multiple-choice tests, for example, are designed to test memory. People who ace these tests may not actually be the most intellectual or involved students—often, great test-takers have terrific memories for short spurts of information, although they may not be able to explain the reasoning behind the correct answers.

So how do these students get by without taking a deep interest in the material? They've simply learned the art of spitting back information via memorization—a skill that *you* can learn if you know just how to handle bits and pieces of data. For example, if someone read a list of ten words or concepts to you, it's unlikely that you would remember all of them. You'd be able to recall most of the things at the beginning, a couple in the middle, and one or two at the end. These effects are known as *primacy* (words or ideas at the beginning) and *recency* (words or ideas at the end).

Primacy and recency are built-in tools that your brain automatically makes available to you. In other words, most people don't struggle with remembering the first or last words in a list, because their memory is programmed to grab hold of them and make them available for recall—it's the items in the middle that will probably give people some trouble.

■ ■

MAKE A MENTALIST NOTE

To take advantage of primacy and recency when you're working on memorizing a list, find a middle ground. If you are doing something that requires a lot of thinking and you work nonstop for hours, you'll find that the dip in the recall between primacy and recency can be quite considerable. If, on the other hand, you stop to take breaks too often, your brain will not really reach primacy, because it keeps on getting interrupted. In short, you might want to try pausing and resting after thirty to fifty minutes of intense work or study, just to give your brain time to refresh itself and to maximize the balance between primacy and recency.

■ ■

MNEMONICS

You'll find that it's easier to recall a word if it's repeated several times in a list, or if it's related to the other words in any way, *or* if it stands out among the other words (for example, the word "ruby" will stand out from a list of vegetables). But the best way to effectively recall all of the words in the list is to use a *mnemonic technique* (mind-memory aid) to help you remember what you've seen or heard.

Association

The most efficient mnemonic technique to remember something is to connect it to something that you already know. The greater the number of associations you can make, the better your chances of recall. Two popular techniques of association are *acronyms* and *acrostics*.

■ An *acronym* is a combination of the first letters of the items to be remembered. For example, an acronym commonly used to remember the sequence of colors in the light spectrum is the name ROY G. BIV: Red, Orange, Yellow, Green, Blue, Indigo, and Violet. Sometimes, the acronym can be more familiar than the complete name itself, such as RAM (Random Access Memory) or SCUBA (Self-Contained Underwater Breathing Apparatus).

■ An *acrostic* is an invented sentence where the first letter of each word is a cue to the thing you want to remember. For example: The phrase "Every Good Boy Deserves Fun" forms an acrostic to remember the order of G-clef notes on sheet music—E, G, B, D, and F. An acrostic for the nine planets of our solar system—Mercury, Venus, Earth, Mars, Jupiter, Saturn, Uranus, Neptune, Pluto—would be "My Very Eager Mother Just Sent Us Nine Peaches."

Visualization and Imagination

Images are visual representations used in memory production. One image can bring words to mind, which can arouse other images. The formation of images appears to help in learning and remembering what has been learned. When used together, images and words are more helpful for remembering things than either one alone.

Let's take a topic like science. Most science books discuss complex concepts that can throw the nonscientific mind for a loop. Fortunately, these books tend to include pictures to depict scientific scenarios that can't be seen by the human eye, like the structure of a bacteria or a virus. Graphic elements and visual tools, therefore, can be used to teach many conceptual scientific ideas.

An investigator might use this particular skill by reading notes about a crime scene and creating vivid images in his or her mind along the way. If the crime scene report described broken glass and blood on the floor, for example, the investigator would stop and "see" this picture, committing it to memory. His or her ability to visualize the scene as it was at the time of the crime will help the investigator when questioning suspects and beginning to put the pieces of the puzzle together.

Here are some methods that you can use to achieve an imaginative memory:

■ Learn to think with both words and pictures. When you're reading a book or a newspaper article, stop and reconstruct the scenario inside your head. You'll improve your recall of the words and also get your memory going. Imagine seeing the destruction after a natural disaster, for example. What do the buildings look like? Can you see areas that have remained untouched, or has everything within sight been destroyed? Are people and animals wandering about or is the area essentially a ghost town?

■ In learning new ideas, associate them with an image or picture that is relevant to you. In other words, use what you already know or what is easily conjured by your brain. When learning the French word for beach, for example, picture your favorite by-the-shore spot and imagine standing there saying, "*la plage, la plage* . . ."

■ If you're reading a technical manual, imagine acting out the scenario spelled out by the book, something called *vivid reading*. Words and sentences come alive with real-life applications.

Clustering

Grouping information is essential in the process of memory retention. Pairing words, for example, either synonymously or with their opposing meanings, like "fair" and "foul" or "man" and "woman," helps us remember words more easily because of the way they give other words meaning.

Remembering words in this way seems easy enough—how about clustering numbers for later recall, though? Seems a little harder, doesn't it? Well, it's pretty commonplace in your world already, like when numbers are grouped into sets of threes and fours, as with telephone numbers. You may not remember a seven-digit number like 5557391, but when it's broken down into two smaller sets—555-7391—suddenly it doesn't seem like an overwhelming task. We'll talk more about how to remember numbers a little later in this chapter.

Sensory Impressions

Did you know that the impressions received from your five senses have a significant role in the retention of information in your mind? This is called Memory of Sense Impressions. And although all of the senses can play a role in the development of memory, if you were to do an analysis of sense impressions, you would find that the majority are acquired through sight and hearing.

Sight Impressions

We are constantly receiving thousands of different sight impressions. Most of these pictures don't make an impression on memory, because we give them little attention or interest. We think that we see things when we look at them, but in reality we see only a few aspects of whatever is in front of us at the moment. Unless you train yourself the right way, you're probably looking at plenty of people, places, and things in your day-to-day life but not truly seeing them. As you can imagine, detectives, police, and other crime-fighters are well versed in using their powers of visual observation anytime, anywhere.

Most of us, however, fall short in this area, even when we really need and try to remember something. For example, eyewitnesses to crimes are notoriously unreliable. One person will report that a mugger was tall, while another reports that he was short. One witness will say that the thief wore red shoes; another will say he was wearing boots. These are usually cases of "looking without seeing." Sometimes events happen so quickly that our mind doesn't have time to catch up to our best intentions . . . unless we've trained ourselves to observe, remember, and report.

The way to train the mind to receive clear sight impressions is simply to focus your attention on objects in your sight, trying to see them plainly and distinctly, and then practice recalling the details of the objects sometime afterward. You can do this with any objects in your home, your office, or outdoors, just as long as you have the time and energy to focus on the details. Look intently at an object or scene for thirty seconds, and then write down everything you can remember about it. Then look again—were your impressions accurate? Is there anything you see the second time around that you missed the first time? Is it a major or minor detail?

Hearing Impressions
The mind will hear the faintest sounds from things in which it has interest, while at the same time ignoring other sounds completely. A sleeping mother will wake up at the slightest cry from

her baby, while she can snooze right through the booming bass from a passing car, her alarm clock, or a barking dog.

Many sounds reach the ear but are not retained by the mind. We walk along a noisy street, and yet the mind accepts the sounds of only a few things, particularly when the novelty of most of the sounds has passed away. This is fine and well in a crowded place, but when it comes time to remembering what was said in a meeting or in a personal conversation, not hearing is often not an excuse. To acquire a better sense of hearing, and the correct memory of things heard, your hearing must be exercised, trained, and developed.

No one can listen to every noise—and it wouldn't be advisable to try—but you can improve your listening skills and commit certain sounds and conversations to memory with the use of your powerful attention. You will find the following techniques helpful:

- Learn to listen more attentively by memorizing words, phrases, or sentences. The next time you're trapped in a conversation at work or at a party (one that you would normally only half-listen to), set your mind on picking out several of the speaker's phrases and, using the powers of imagery we discussed earlier, allow those phrases to make an impression on your mind. (You'll be surprised and impressed with yourself when you can remember even the dullest conversations with ease.)

- Listen to the tiny bits of dialogue you hear while walking on the street, and aim to memorize a sentence or two, as if you're going to retell them to a friend. Study the expressions and inflections in the voices of persons speaking around you. You will be astonished at the impression that this will make on your mind.

■ Have a friend read a couple lines of poetry to you and then you try to memorize them. Keep doing this and you will significantly develop your power of voluntary attention to sounds and spoken words. But above everything else, practice repeating the words and sounds that you have memorized, as many times as possible. By doing this, you will get your mind into the habit of taking an interest in sound impressions.

The Two-in-One Method

In some cases the impressions of sight and sound are joined together, as when you read. The sound and shape of the letters are stored away in your memory together. When this combination takes place, the memory in question is far more readily recalled than things of which only one sense impression is recorded.

Teachers help their students to remember words by having them speaking the words aloud and then write them down. People can also memorize names, events, or concepts in this way, thus doubling the potential for recall. This is why some students, for example, find it very helpful to study with a friend or a group. The information is written in front of them, but discussing the ideas—hearing them bantered about the room—gives the information a whole new dimension when it's committed to memory. This method can also help to improve a "weaker sense"—that is, if you can usually recall what you've read or seen but you can't ever seem to remember what you've heard, then discussing what you've read or seen will link that information to your "ear memory," which not only gives you another memory resource to call on, but also strengthens your hearing memory for future use. You'll note that the characters in *The Mentalist* can often be found talking about the crime scene, their suspects, and their theories about what's happened. That's part and parcel of police work, and it helps to underscore the most important aspects of each case.

More Complex Memory

When Patrick Jane begins observing the world around him and those in it, we see him removed from the situation—he allows himself to plunge into a sensory state to better increase his ability to remember information. However, some of the displays of his flawless mind leave even memory experts scratching their heads. His ability to remember large volumes of seemingly unrelated numbers seems almost like a magic trick. But there's no magic involved—just smart thinking!

In "Red Handed," Patrick wins a lot of money at the casino and admits it's because he was counting cards. His coworkers can't believe he's actually able to remember the placement of all of the cards in the deck, but he explains that he can do so because he makes the cards a part of his "memory palace." Patrick explains that it's "a place so clear in your mind that you can walk all around it in your head. Everyone's palace is different, but it has to be big and detailed and vivid."

Another term for the memory palace technique is the Method of Loci. It's actually a device that's been used for centuries, often for remembering long speeches. Many credit the Ancient Greek poet and orator Simonides of Ceos with originating this mnemonic device. As the story goes, Simonides had been entertaining at a large dinner when he ducked out of the building for a few minutes and the entire banquet hall collapsed. The catastrophe left many of the dead unrecognizable to family and loved ones. So Simonides aided recovery efforts by identifying the dead based entirely on where he remembered they'd been seated during his performance. In order to accomplish this, he used the Method of Loci.

I'm going to show you how to build your own memory palace, one brick at a time.

THE MEMORY PALACE

The key to building your memory palace is to make sure you're basing it on a place that you know like the back of your hand. Maybe it's your home, the house you grew up in, or the place where you work. Maybe it's even based on the route you drive to work every day. Whatever the case, you should be able to picture this place very clearly and vividly imagine yourself walking from room to room, or traveling each inch of the drive, remembering each landmark in detail.

Now you'll need to connect the list of things you have to remember with the places in your memory palace that you know so well. For instance, let's say you need to remember your shopping list for the hardware store: a can of red paint, paintbrushes, a shovel, potting soil, and a hammer. If you've based your memory palace on your home, you may think of your front door first. This one's easy. Imagine red paint splashed all over the door. When you enter the house you see a staircase in front of you. You imagine the paintbrushes dancing on the stairs, the bristles shaped like little legs kicking up and down. I know this sounds ridiculous, but the more outlandish the images you create, the more likely it is you'll be able to remember them later. After you've walked past the stairs, you enter the kitchen. Imagine your husband using a garden shovel to eat a bowl of cereal. As you pass him, you'll look into the bathroom and see that the bathtub is filled with dirt. And finally you'll walk into the living room and find that your remote control has been smashed with a hammer.

It may take a bit of time to commit these images to memory at first. But as you get to know your memory palace better, this method will get easier and take less time to construct.

THE LINK METHOD

I learned the Link Method from the books of Harry Lorayne. Harry is a legendary magician and memory-training specialist who appeared on *The Tonight Show Starring Johnny Carson*. He wrote several successful books on mnemonic techniques, including *The Memory Book* (cowritten by Jerry Lucas), which was a huge *New York Times* bestseller .

With this technique, you remember your list by using imagery to link each item with the one directly before and after it. Let's say your list is the following:

- George Washington

- John Adams

- Thomas Jefferson

To remember Washington, you associate his name with washing. The name Adams may remind you of a man's adam's apple. So for the first link you see a man with soap and water, washing his throat, with a prominent Adam's apple. Perhaps the name Jefferson reminds you of one of your favorite bands of the sixties, Jefferson Airplane. So you can then imagine watching a man with an enormous Adam's apple singing Jefferson Airplane's "Somebody to Love."

Obviously, these images wouldn't work for every person. Everyone has to find the associations that work best for him or her. In fact, after trying several of these memory techniques, you may devise a unique method that works best for you. The system I use is actually a combination of several techniques. Let me share the story of one of my performances to demonstrate the method I've found works best for me.

SIMON'S MEMORY METHOD AND THE PEG SYSTEM

A few years ago I was invited to entertain at Icehotel in Jukkas-järvi, Sweden. It's truly a magnificent place, with everything made of ice and snow—I even slept on a bed of ice. The shows that I performed there were certainly career highlights for me.

One of my nights at Icehotel I used my memory technique to amaze the audience. I asked a group to gather around and to start naming objects. They could choose anything: people (living or dead), places, or things. This was a creative group. They didn't come up with run-of-the-mill, ordinary things. They each tried to outdo the others with their ingenuity.

Before we go into their list of objects, let me first tell you a little bit about how I remember the order of these lists. I use something known as the "peg system." This is a method very effective for memorizing lists. You create "peg words" to represent numbers and sequencing. In this instance, I needed to remember a list of twenty objects. So first I associated each of the numbers one through twenty with an image. The easiest way to do this is to compare the sound of the number to another word that phonetically resembles it. So what's a word that sounds like "one"? Something else may pop into your mind first, and if so, that's the image you should use, but personally, I think of the word "gun." Here's a list of the word I associate with each number from one to twenty. Most of these words are commonly used for this mnemonic system.

1= gun	11=Leavenworth Prison
2= shoe	12=hell
3= tree	13=hurting
4= door	14=farting
5= hive	15=fitting
6= sticks	16=sitting
7= heaven	17= seven canteens
8= gate	18=waiting
9= wine	19=lightning
10=hen	20=penny

Go over this list in your mind. You may not be able to commit all the words to memory right away. The ones that will probably be easiest for you to recall are those that rhyme naturally. If there are a few that just don't seem to be sticking in your head, this might be a sign that you need to figure out your own association for that number.

To further solidify the images in my mind, I also use them as part of my memory palace. Each number and the object that will go with it is associated with part of the pathway to my home in Las Vegas. By associating these images to objects that are specific to me, I make it much easier for me to remember associations. It's difficult to make the peg system work if you're not using visuals that are very familiar to you. Here's how it works:

1= gun = There is a street sign in front of the condo I live in, and I imagine a huge gun pointed right at the sign.

2= shoe = When I drive up to my complex, the last thing I do before getting out of my car is pull my foot off the pedal. One time I kicked my shoe off after a long day's work and it felt *good*! So I mentally picture my shoe sitting by itself in the car, looking kind of lonely.

3= tree = There is a large tree on the way to the front door of my building.

4= door = This is an easy one. I picture the front door of my building.

5= hive = When I go through the door of my building, there is a buzzer system. The sound reminds me of a beehive, so as I walk through to the vestibule of my condo, I imagine myself wading through a huge beehive.

6= sticks = I love hardwood floors and the noise you can make walking across them. For this association, I imagine beating on the floors with drumsticks, like a toddler.

7= heaven = I envision the elevator doors in my building. When I wait for them to open, it's like waiting for the gates of heaven to open to me.

8= gate = This is the gate I enter to actually get to my condo.

9= wine = At the top floor when the elevator opens, there is a bottle of wine sitting on the floor waiting for me.

10=hen = As the elevator doors open when it reaches my floor, I see a jumbo hen there to greet me.

11=Leavenworth Prison = There's a long walkway to my unit and I imagine it as the long hallway to a cell in the prison.

12=hell = I imagine that opening my front door is like opening the door to hell.

13=hurting = One time I hit my elbow against the frame of the door as I entered, and well—ouch.

14=farting = Well, right past the front door of my condo is the bathroom. Enough said.

15=fitting = Next, I walk into my bedroom and think about how I try to fit into my old clothes after gaining some weight. But when I imagine it, I exaggerate the situation to a cartoonlike level.

16=sitting = My meditation area is in my bedroom, so I can see myself there.

17=7 canteens = I often bring bottles of water into my bedroom and forget to finish them, so they tend to sit on my window-sill. I picture seven there.

18=waiting = I'm often waiting in my bedroom for my girlfriend to hurry up and get ready.

19=lightning = I'll admit that there was a night when a thunderstorm outside my bedroom window gave me a bit of a fright. I can still see the flashes of lightning.

20=penny = I have a large penny that sits on my desk.

So now that you're armed with a way to remember the order of this list, you can move on to the next step, which leads me to the list of objects I received from my audience at the Icehotel. It went something like this:

Rabbit	Ted Nugent
Dog	Calendar
James Bond	Red purse
Purple	$53
Porsche Boxter	Gymnastics
Laptop	Dubai
Vanilla Sky	Ladder
Skeleton	Silver balloon
Museum	Flat-screen TV
Rhinoceros	1983

To commit these items to memory in the correct order, I created images that associated the number peg words to the items on the list. Some of these connections may seem strange or morose, but I just use what works best for me. And remember, it's usually best to go with the most outlandish image you can conjure. It's easier to remember craziness than anything that's ho-hum.

1. Rabbit—I see a huge white rabbit holding the large gun that's shooting at my street sign.

2. Dog—There is a Doberman sitting in my car, wearing my shoes and trying to press the gas pedals.

3. James Bond—Sean Connery is standing under the tree at my building. He greets me and says, "My name is Bond. James Bond."

4. Purple—I once performed for Robert Downey, Jr. He commented on the purple suit I was wearing. So I picture Iron Man in a purple suit as the doorman of my building.

5. Porsche Boxter—I see the car crashing through the glass entryway of my building, setting off the buzzer. And billions of bees escape out of their large hive in the vestibule.

6. Laptop—I'm wearing laptops as my shoes and the sound they make against the hardwood floor is like the sound of the drumsticks beating.

7. Vanilla Sky—As the elevator doors open, I look up to heaven and see a vanilla sky.

8. Skeleton—The elevator gate opens and there is a skeleton there. Someone was waiting a *long time* to get upstairs.

9. Museum—When I see the bottle of wine waiting for me, it reminds me of a fancy party I once attended at a museum.

10. Rhinoceros—As the elevator opens and I see the hen, I hear a rhinoceros charging down the hallway. He eats the hen and I barely escape.

11. Ted Nugent—Well, sorry Ted, but I picture him in shackles, walking the long corridor in Leavenworth Prison.

12. Calendar—I see a calendar hanging on my door to hell, telling me my days are numbered.

13. Purse—As I open my door, there's a woman waiting for me and she hits me over the head with her big, red purse. Jeez—what did I do?

14. $53—My friends make a rather disgusting bet about who can fart the loudest. They wager $53.

15. Gymnastics—It takes some gymnastics to get into a tight leotard while trying to keep up with a Richard Simmons workout.

16. Dubai—In my meditation area, I'm sitting on a globe. I'm positioned directly over Dubai.

17. Ladder—I see the 7 canteens/water bottles stacked on my windowsill like the steps of a ladder.

18. Silver balloon—As I watch my girlfriend doing her hair, a large silver balloon floats in and carries her away.

19. Flat-screen TV—The lightning from that awful storm strikes my TV and it explodes.

20. 1983—I see a bunch of 1983 pennies on my desk, and they are arranged to form the number 1983.

Some of these images may come to your mind naturally, but a lot of them probably seem off-the-wall. Since we all have our quirks and our own personal experiences, each of our associations will probably seem kind of weird or funny to anybody else. You have to create the memory palace and elaborate system that works for you.

As crazy as some of my imagery might sound, it helped me to remember the list those audience members gave me at Icehotel. I was able to remember their items and repeat them back in perfect order.

And just remember . . .

The better aware we become of *how* we build a system of information, the better that system becomes in performing tasks such as memorization or application of memory. In other words, everyone is different, and the memorization skills that work well for one person may not work as well for you.

Some tips to begin:

▪ Learn to analyze situations, details, experiences. Try to extract the relevant facts and remove unnecessary data or information.

▪ Know your capacity for the process of memorization. Are you the type of person who easily gets the information by clustering it into meaningful categories, or are you the type of person who learns better if you follow directions or a picture inside your head? Use what works for you!

Don't become discouraged if you are not a Mentalist by tomorrow! Much of this is very individualized, and although anyone can improve his or her memory, it takes dedication and, sometimes, trial and error.

CHAPTER THREE

The Mentalist's Eye: Observing the Details

We've all seen the news stories about innocent men and women who've been convicted based on mistaken eyewitness accounts. According to the Innocence Project—an organization dedicated to exonerating the wrongfully accused and reforming the judicial system—eyewitness misidentification has played a role in more that 75 percent of convictions that were later overturned with DNA evidence.

A lot of factors can cause these cases of mistaken identity: poor visibility, faulty witness instruction, and unreliable memory, to name a few. But there's an underlying truth here: that most of us just aren't really paying attention to everything around us all of the time. We're just not programmed to be observant. It's difficult to remember something if you never really and truly gave it a good look in the first place.

Patrick Jane isn't your average eyewitness. Few details get by him unnoticed. He's able to see and take note of things that most people would not give a second thought.

Engaging All of the Senses

In truth, a mentalist needs more than just a keen eye. A mentalist must rely on *all* of the senses to take in the complete picture.

In Episode 16 of Season 1 of *The Mentalist* ("Bloodshot"), Jane is blinded by an accident and has to wear bandages over his eyes for the entire episode, but that doesn't stop him from having an uncanny ability to read people and understand the situation around him. In fact, in a blind state, Jane probably has stronger observation skills than most of us have with full use of our sight and all other senses. We often use our eyes as a crutch.

In the "Bloodshot" episode Jane truly is blind, albeit for a short amount of time. But mentalists around the world often use their powers of observation to wow a crowd by covering their eyes and reading the person or the situation in front of them.

The next time you're at a party, take a moment to test the observations of all of your senses. You may see a lot of men in suits and ties, and women wearing high heels and cocktail dresses. Perhaps you see a bar with a line of people waiting for refreshments.

At the same time what do you hear? No doubt there are conversations going on all around you. But if you ignore those for a moment, can you hear the pop of the bartender opening a new bottle of wine? The traffic outside the building? The shuffle of tired feet on the hardwood floors?

What smells can you pick up? The hors d'oeuvres have probably been calling to you all night. But can you smell the perfume of the woman standing next to you? Can you catch a whiff of the cleaning products that were most likely used to make the space suitable for company?

When you taste the appetizers, can you discern some of the ingredients? Can you identify the type of wine you're drinking beyond just whether it's red or white?

Finally, when you shook another partygoer's hand, did you note the coarseness of his palm? When a woman's skirt brushed by your legs, could you detect the type of fabric?

If we rely solely on our eyes, we miss out on all of these other observations and potential opportunities to learn about people. So let's imagine you are walking in Patrick Jane's shoes. You have been presented with an object as evidence. Do you think that Jane might somewhere in the back of his mind take a moment to remember the Sherlock Holmes scenario so well crafted in *The Sign of Four* and use his super-keen skills of observation to begin unlocking the hidden secrets of the object?

Unlocking the Clues

So much of this book will be about readings or, as I said, the ability to meet someone or hold an object for the first time and instantly uncover loads of information about either one.

Often Jane will win over some skeptical person with his ability to make seemingly instant decisions about them. That is a stock-in-trade tool of the mentalist.

Sure, you might feel a little odd using mentalist skills that have been culled from the world of fake psychics and mediums—such as cold readings (more on cold readings in Chapter 7)—but don't think of these abilities as fraudulent. In fact, the mentalist's toolbox may be most notably exhibited by one of the world's most celebrated literary figures—and a purveyor of justice. Many of the techniques used by Jane and outlined in this book are examples of observation and deduction that have been pulled from the pages of none other than Sherlock Holmes.

In the opening scene of Sir Arthur Conan Doyle's *The Sign of Four* Dr. Watson hands Holmes a recently inherited pocket watch—with the challenge that Holmes describe the character of its late owner.

After a brief pause Holmes concludes that the watch probably belonged to Watson's older brother.

"Your brother was a man of untidy habits, very untidy and careless," says Holmes. "He was left with good prospects but threw away his chances, lived for some time in poverty with occasional short bursts of prosperity and finally turning to drink he died."

Holmes was right!

Many times we see Patrick Jane presented with an object—most memorably, and grotesquely, with a severed appendage, in

"Red-Handed"—and somehow out of nowhere he'll be able to reveal information about the object's history and its owner, much like the stories of Holmes and Watson. Sometimes a mentalist can incorporate conversation and environment when reading an object. But other times he or she doesn't have the luxury of that extra information and must rely on just the object itself.

This is how Jane does it:

Let's go back to that severed hand in "Red-Handed." The show opens with our investigative team studying a grisly discovery on the highway. It's pretty evident that this is a man's hand, and the number "43" has been written on the palm. Getting down on all fours to take a look at it, Jane makes several observations about the hand and even smells it. That's right; I said he smells the severed hand. You must make use of all your senses.

Since the ink is faded and the markings are so small, Jane declares that it's unlikely the number forty-three was placed there by the murderer. Therefore, it was most likely written by the victim himself. The number's written on his right hand, so it's reasonable to assume that the victim was left-handed.

With his sense of smell, Jane detects the scent of an almond oil moisturizer, tobacco, and musky cologne. He also notes that the deceased had professionally manicured hands and soft palms. All of this adds up to a wealthy victim.

Finally, Patrick directs their attention to a faint tan line on the pinky finger. Clearly the victim had worn a ring there. Generally speaking, Jane says, pinky rings denote an extrovert.

After what most would think was an extensive, if somewhat bizarre, assessment of the hand, Jane proclaims that it belongs to someone who is "upper management in a hotel or gaming business."

One of the CBI agents, Kimball Cho, doubts the mentalist's ability to deduce all of that by simply sniffing and looking at the appendage and agrees to a meager thirty-five-cent bet claiming that Jane is wrong.

Never bet against Patrick Jane. Of course, he turns out to be exactly right. It wouldn't be much of a television show if he wasn't, now would it?

But this isn't just a case of some made-for-TV magic. Jane's deductions are actually quite reasonable and realistic. I can prove it by presenting you with another example. Let's say the object that you're being asked to read is a simple silver watch. How would you accomplish that? Do you have the skills? You will.

And so let us begin. Come with me as I open up my secrets, first with the art of reading objects and then into the deeper, more astute world of being a mentalist.

Take a Second to Stop, Think, Observe

Take a second to think about what you would deduce from an object sitting in front of you.

In this case, it's a silver watch. What story does it tell?

There are simple observations that you can make. In the past, you probably would've taken these things for granted or simply wouldn't have taken the opportunity to stop and observe. Is the watch shiny or dull? Does it look tarnished? Does it appear to be worn down on one side more than the other? Is there anything on it, any markings that would help uncover a time period?

All of these observations can help you determine the source of this watch and the description of the person it belongs to.

Take all the time you need to look at the watch. Don't speak too quickly, because once you start there's no going back.

Let's say you notice that there are some areas where you can see that the watch has been rubbed against surfaces, but at the same time it's shiny. If it's been worn down from use that shows it's a favorite piece of the subject's, so much so that she took the time to shine it and keep it looking pretty. If it's a favorite piece, perhaps it was given as a gift or is a family heirloom.

If this is a blind reading and you don't have the person in front of you, you can look to see how long or short the watch is, signifying the width of the owner's wrist. Narrower wrists naturally point to more petite people. So you can make that connection as well.

What colors or shapes are on the watch? You often can connect colors with someone's general mood. Lighter colors may be worn by someone who is generally more pleasant and optimistic, while darker colors could highlight a more pessimistic personality.

So far, just from holding this watch, we potentially could say that its owner is a petite woman, who received the watch as a gift (heirlooms also can be considered gifts). She considers this watch one of her favorite pieces of jewelry and wears it often. And she has a happy demeanor.

All that, and we never even met the person. Let's dig deeper.

Observations alone won't uncover all of the clues. You have to study! You need to use context.

If you've done your homework, you'll already know how certain items worn by left-hand-dominant people will wear out in a different location than the same item worn by a right-hand-dominant person. Hold the watch with the top to the left and the opening or clasp to the right. Now examine the pattern of wear and tarnish on the inside of the watch. If we see that there is tarnish on the lower interior and that the upper interior is buffed clean, we can deduce that the watch was worn on the left wrist, because the natural oils of the skin caused a chemical reaction darkening the interior of the watch, but the constant friction of the upper interior section against the skin of the wrist caused the discoloration to wear away, thus it must have been worn on the left wrist. We might further deduce that if the watch was worn on the left wrist, and this woman is not wearing a wristwatch on her right wrist, then she is probably right-handed.

In the same way, if you've studied, you'll have learned that glasses with a narrow frame likely belong to someone with a narrower head, and people with narrower heads tend to be shorter than people with wider heads. You'll recognize the way a shoe appears when it's been worn by one type of person as opposed to another.

These types of useful observations are endless, and so they can be difficult to teach. They're better learned through years of patient observation. You have to study people every day to pick up on all of these idiosyncrasies, understanding that you'll be able to use them later to read certain objects.

■ ■

MENTALIST OBSERVATION EXERCISE
A Picture's Worth a Thousand Words

This is a great exercise to perform with a group of aspiring mentalists.

Choose a "busy" photo from a magazine and let everyone take a turn writing down as many details about that picture as possible. If you'd like to set a time limit, you can, but it's really important to give each person enough time to study the photo thoroughly.

Once everyone has had a turn, compare your observations with one another. Did your friends catch things that you didn't? Think about why you may have missed certain things, and how you can train yourself to be more attentive next time.

■ ■

Now what if we have the person in front of us and are able to incorporate some of that into our observations?

Observing People

So like I said, we were able to come up with all of that information without even seeing anyone in front of us. But what if we also were able to utilize observations gained through watching someone standing in front us and how that person interacts with the surrounding environment? That could provide for more detailed and accurate observations.

Clues about people are literally all over them. We can tell if someone is wearing contact lenses by paying close attention to the pressure and stress immediately beneath the eyelid. Contacts cause the skin beneath the eyelid to be more taut or stretched in appearance.

Looking at a person's shoes will tell you a fair amount about that person. Are they scuffed? Is there dirt on them? Could they be a work shoe?

Are they expensive shoes? If you don't feel comfortable making that kind of assessment, visit the shoe department of various stores the next time you're shopping. Learn to differentiate between the materials, styles, and finishes found at Kmart and compare them to those at Neiman Marcus or another high-end store. Spend some time getting to know the signature looks of the expensive designers.

One time I was approached by a saleswoman who commented that I would look great in a pair of Gucci loafers. I tried them on—and they were amazing—but then I found out the price. Almost $500. Wow! Well, you can bet I never forgot those loafers, and so when I later saw them on a gentleman in my audience, I called him out on them. I knew that most people who invest in shoes like those are comfortable with—and sometimes even seek—attention. So my observation told me a lot about his financial status and his personality.

You truly need to dissect the person in front of you.

Look at the person's hands. Are there calluses? If there are, what does that tell you? You probably can assume the person either works with his or her hands or frequently lift weights. If the person isn't in great shape, you can rule out the weight lifting.

How about their nails: Are they neatly groomed or bitten? Personally, I hate the fact that I bite my nails. I know all too well that it's a sign of nervousness, and it often means that whoever does it is skittish about something going on in his or her life. I tend to leave my nails alone when I'm in a "good place": relaxed, calm, and focused.

Skin tone can be a good indicator too. It can tell you a bit about the person's heritage or nationality. Or perhaps it signifies that the person is a "sun worshipper." Those who love the sun and have spent copious hours in it will have crow's-feet in addition to the darker skin tone. Your subject is likely an outdoor worker or someone who "has it all" and spends lots of time at the beach.

Or does that tan look more man-made than sun-kissed? If you suspect the person has a spray tan, you can make the assumption that that person is very concerned with his or her appearance.

If a woman is wearing a rather eye-catching, crazy outfit—like hot pants or a loud print—you can deduce that she's either the artistic type or a little behind in the current fashions. Low-cut blouses and short skirts often mean that the woman is comfortable with her body. And if she's wearing panty hose, you might consider if it's because she's going for a conservative, corporate look, or because she's anxious about exposing her legs.

We can tell if people are right- or left-handed by the way they fasten their belt, tie a tie, or wear a watch, or simply by paying attention to which hand is favored while they talk and gesture.

Then you can take this information one step further. Since left- and right-hand dominance are an indication of brain function, we can make some assumptions about the subject's personality based on this tidbit. Only one out of every ten people is left-handed, so it can be easier and more appropriate to use the general information we have on that small population to really deepen a reading. Unlike the rest of us, who think more from the left side—known as the more rational side—of our brains, lefties rely more on the creative side. They tend to be more artistic and musical, and to be out-of-the-box thinkers.

Lefties have been getting a bad rap for centuries. Even the Bible reads more favorably for the right hand. You won't find a reference anywhere that refers to the "left hand of God" being the place of honor. Most everyday tools are geared toward righties too. Lefties have to use special scissors, can openers, and corkscrews, or program themselves to do it right-handed. Nevertheless, some of world's best and brightest are lefties. Bill Clinton, Ghandi, Robert Redford, Mark Twain, Kurt Cobain, and Jimi Hendrix were all "southpaws."

So how can we use this information to our advantage? Well, by using some of the things we know about the different sides of the brain, we can make generalizations about the left-handed person's life. For instance, a reading for a left-handed person could go something like this:

> "I believe you have a strong independent character and my sense is you have strong ties to family. You have a generous soul and worry a bit about not doing enough for others. I see you starting some kind of a creative endeavor. Perhaps writ-

ing? I'm not seeing this clearly . . . What is your hobby or the artistic project you gave up years ago, but wish to return to?"

Remember to try not to ask too many direct yes-or-no questions, because if you're a mind reader, then you are supposed to have all the answers. Instead, lead with the information you have and wait for the person to fill in the details. Then always end the reading with some positive statements to leave your subject content.

Considering all of these questions and potential observations can seem almost intimidating to the new or novice mentalist, but it's completely necessary. While the act of object reading can offer us some excellent information about a subject, there's nothing like reading the person standing in front of us, and all that the person comes with. Separately, each observation you make might not leave you confident in your reading ability, but by taking all of the information about the object and the person, including the clues the person wears every day, you can piece together an accurate and crowd-pleasing assessment.

READING FACES

Much of the work I do as a mentalist is based on microexpressions, or brief, involuntary facial expressions. By interpreting them, I can gain a fuller understanding of my subject. A micro-expression is the minute muscle movements you make when you have a lot at stake and can't control the movement of your mouth, eyes, or brow.

■ ■

MENTALIST MENTOR

Patrick Jane most certainly studies micro-expressions when he's questioning a suspect, but the technique is even more notably practiced by the character Dr. Cal Lightman on the hit Fox show *Lie to Me*. In the series, Lightman is known as the world's leading deception expert and uses a lot of the same observations Jane uses in a much more obvious and scientific manner. Micro-expressions certainly take the spotlight on that program.

These involuntary expressions were first discovered and discussed more than forty years ago. Paul Ekman—whom Dr. Cal Lightman is loosely based on—has spent much of his career researching and cataloging these "tells" and is considered a preeminent expert and pioneer on the subject. His studies far surpass what we as mentalists need to know.

■ ■

In Chapter 4 I cover eye-accessing cues in more detail, which is essentially all that you really need to know as a mentalist when dealing with micro-expressions and lie detection. Eye-accessing cues give you a reading on what someone is thinking based on the person's eye movements when he or she speaks. For instance, depending on if a subject looks up, down, or forward, you can determine whether that person is accessing a visual, audible, or emotional memory or thought. It's actually quite an effective mentalist tool when mastered.

Patrick Jane knows very well that the eyes are the windows to the soul. When asked how he knows that a suspect is telling the truth, and is indeed innocent of a murder, he says matter-of-factly, "It's in her eyes."

The general theory on micro-expressions is that they can reveal seven distinct emotions: happiness, fear, sadness, contempt, anger, disgust, and surprise. They can be fast, almost too fast to notice, or much more deliberate and telling.

Here are some basic ways to pick up on these seven key emotions through micro-expressions:

- Happiness—When people are happy they smile, right? It's not too difficult to fake a smile, though some of us fake them better than others. But the true way to identify whether someone is happy is to look at his or her eyes. Do they develop crow's-feet when the person smiles, and does the skin around the eyes move? If not, that smile is fake.

- Fear—Identify fear by looking at lips, eyes, and eyebrows. Look for for lips to stretch horizontally toward the ears and for eyebrows to rise. A frightened person's eyelids also will be tensed and raised.

- Sadness—Also look to the eyes when looking for signs of sadness or depression. If someone's eyelids and eyebrows droop, that person is likely sad. Also look for a general lack of focus in the eyes. A pouty lip also is hard to fake.

■ Contempt—If you see movement only on one side of someone's face, that's contempt. If the lips on the left half of the face move, maybe even looking like they have a twitch, that's contempt. The giveaway movement could be as subtle as lip movement or as obvious a full tilt of the head.

■ Anger—When angry, people tend to focus their eyes and eyelids downward. The eye movement is a subtle sign of anger, while you also might spot the obvious snarl of the mouth.

■ Disgust—Disgust can be identified by observing someone's upper lip and nose. If the upper lip curls upward, exposing the teeth, that's disgust. It often will be accompanied by a crinkling of the nose.

Like I said, micro-expressions aren't always easy to identify. They often happen too quickly for the novice mentalist to pick up on, but they're also invaluable, because only someone with an exceedingly strong will and brain power can react to a high-stress situation without offering up one of these micro-expressions for you to read.

Investigating Further

Now that we've learned how to use all of our senses to note the clues in objects and people alike, we can delve deeper. Observation is a key step in any investigative or scientific process. Without keen observation, we don't know what questions to ask or what conclusions to make. That's why it's so important to be thorough and accurate.

Let's see how our observations can help uncover the truth.

CHAPTER FOUR

Lies, Lies, Lies

"Lies are often much more plausible, more appealing to reason, than reality, since the liar has the great advantage of knowing beforehand what the audience wishes or expects to hear."

— HANNAH ARENDT

What if you could tell when someone was lying? How could you use that skill in your daily life? How about in the boardroom? What about when buying a car?

Do I really need that undercoat protection and that additional wax?

And we've all heard that joke about lawyers: "How can you tell when a lawyer is lying? His mouth is moving."

Seriously though, having the ability to acknowledge and deal with a deceptive person can be one of the most powerful weapons in your life. It will help you improve your relationships, work life, and daily interactions. This knowledge also is very useful for managers, employers, and for anyone to use in everyday situations where telling the truth from a lie can help prevent you from being a victim of fraud, scams, and other deceptions.

* * *

Patrick Jane has the uncanny ability to instantly tell whether a person is being honest or deceptive. This largely comes from his abilities in "intuitive observation," by which he comes to conclusions based on not only the world around him, but also how those around him are acting.

To become a real-life mentalist, you will eventually allow these separate techniques to fuse seamlessly in your mind, allowing you at a moment's notice to call upon all of the valuable ideas, concepts, and techniques I am sharing in this book.

The techniques employed by Patrick Jane when he is determining if someone is telling the truth are often used by private investigators and police officers to determine if someone is lying, as, for example, when someone is faking being under hypnosis.

LIE DETECTION—CURSE OR BLESSING?

Do you really want to know every time someone is lying to you? You might not. Sometimes ignorance is bliss. After gaining the ability to tell truth from a lie, you may be hurt when it is obvious that someone is lying to you. Once you turn this ability on—there is no off switch.

Types of Liars

Before we can learn how to read when someone is lying, we need to understand that there are several different types of liars out there.

You may remember overhearing a friend in your grade school class tell another friend that he or she was a "compulsive liar." Kids say a lot of things they don't understand, but the truth is there are many people who at a very early age develop patterns of being compulsive liars, which means simply lying out of habit.

Here are the different types of liars you might encounter over your days:

■ Compulsive liars—Compulsive liars lie out of habit, and it feels very natural to them. They tell lies both big and small, and often their habitual lying stems from some childhood environment where lying was a necessity.

■ Pathological liars—While compulsive liars are habitual liars and simply make lying part of their lifestyle, pathological liars are defined as people who incessantly lie to get their way. They're more concerned with manipulating a situation then the compulsive liar is.

■ Occasional liars—As I'll say again later, everyone lies. Some of us lie frequently and others occasionally, to try to get out of a sticky situation. Often these occasional lies stem from some sort of fear of punishment.

- Professional liars—These are your car salesmen and attorneys. No! I'm not calling every car salesman and attorney a liar, but there are certain people out there whose job it is to lie to you to make a sale or advance a business. Whether it be in the boardroom or at the grocery store, these people are trying to sell you something and will stop at nothing to do it.

Patrick Jane is a professional liar himself. In his rather checkered past, he used those lies to defraud people who were gullible enough to believe him. Since the murder of his family, however, he uses his "powers of deception" for the better good at the California Bureau of Investigation. He's found a way to use lies to get to the truth. And who would make a better lie detector than someone who's an expert at lying himself?

Training Your Radar

We all think we have a pretty good radar for picking up on when someone is lying. We call it our BS radar, don't we? Sometimes it's a gut reaction. Other times we pick up on lies based on the way someone says something, or that person's body language.

We all have an innate ability to pick up on when someone is lying. The cues are there, and like I said, often we are able to pick up on them without even realizing it.

But what if you knew exactly what to look for? What if you knew that when someone looked in one direction he or she was recalling a memory, but if that person looked in the opposite direction he or she was trying to imagine a scene that hadn't yet occurred? Would that serve as a useful tool to you? Of course it would.

Well all of that is available to us.

PHYSICAL EXPRESSIONS

Picking up on a person's physical expressions is the most common way to detect a lie.

Again, it is important to remember that no single one of these indicators will lead us to lie detection, but through allowing these techniques to come together and form your own "intuitive observation," you can become a real mentalist. However, if you notice someone constantly touching his or her face, especially covering the mouth or touching the nose, these are strong indicators of that person being concerned about telling a lie. These nonverbal signals, when combined with other basic observations, allow us to begin to form a strong conclusion that maybe someone is not being as honest with us as we might hope.

Start out by using your peripheral vision and watch for changes in a person's body language as that person speaks to you. The great thing about the "peripheral peek," as we call it, is that you don't have to stare directly at the person.

First use these methods of observation to determine whether someone is open to communicating with you or closed off. What is the person's current state of mind? Specifically watch for a shift in position as someone either moves closer or farther away from you. A tilting of the head or leaning forward is also an indicator of how willing a person is to engage with you.

When your subject draws closer to you in any way, this is an obvious and definite clue that he or she is accepting and responding favorably to whatever it is that you are saying or doing. Nodding is another clear sign of agreement and acceptance.

If your subject seems closed off or frustrated, or is not acknowledging you—perhaps fiddling with a phone or keys—that person doesn't want to tell you what he or she is thinking and will likely lie to you or withhold information. A change in breathing pattern or frowning and scrunching up the forehead can also signify that someone is not comfortable interacting with you.

Oftentimes when a person is lying, his or her anxiety about the situation will result in an increase in pulse rate and blood pressure. Patrick Jane will often touch a subject's wrist. The suspect is often a little freaked out, but that's not really relevant. Patrick's already obtained the information he needed. If the pulse is "thread," he knows the person is being deceptive.

Some of us might not be comfortable grabbing a person's wrist every time we think someone may be lying. But there are more visible indicators of an increase in blood pressure. For most people this manifests in a flushed skin tone. In the episode "Redwood," Patrick points out that a suspect blushed when he obviously lied about his weight. Sometimes this reddening or pinkness is easily spotted in the wrist and hand area if it isn't as obvious in the subject's face. Similarly, body temperature changes are great clues as to whether someone is telling you the truth. If a person suddenly gets very hot and sweaty or decides that he or she suddenly needs a sweatshirt, something is amiss.

You'll notice that if someone is lying, his or her physical expression will be hindered or stifled a bit. The liar takes up less space, with limited movement of arms and hands. Nobody wants to stick out like a sore thumb when being deceptive. It's human nature to want to blend into the background when we have something to hide. We try to occupy as small a space as possible, hoping that we will not be noticed; much like the child who covers his eyes and scrunches up into a ball beneath his blanket to make himself invisible to the imaginary monster under the bed.

Therefore, if you notice someone becoming dramatically less imposing in his or her frame, this is a good sign that the person is lying.

While none of these things alone will give you 100 percent accuracy, they are the very first steps. When looking for the truth, these should be the first port of call before moving on to the other areas of attention and interest.

■ ■

FACT OR MYTH

A person who is lying to you will often avoid eye contact.
That's a *myth*!

One of the major myths about someone telling a lie is the notion that such a person does not look you in the eye. While this seems logical, it is in most cases incorrect. You see, people often will know this myth and will therefore act in accordance with what they think someone being truthful would do. They will often hold strong eye contact and will not break this for a moment. Studies have been done on pupil dilation while telling lies, but a dilated pupil has been proven to be inconclusive evidence in detecting a lie. When someone displays no movement in the eyes, however, it is normally a good indication of that person being untruthful.

■ ■

EMOTIONAL GESTURES

Another great indication of deception can be the timing and presentation of a subject's emotional reaction to your cue. Liars' reactions are often delayed, and when they eventually do react their response seems forced and contorted. Then the reaction vanishes again with inappropriate timing.

The flow of a conversation is often dictated by the truthfulness of the content contained therein. If we think about information that is true as being instant to access, always on hand, and easy to retrieve, and deceptive information as being created in the moment, we begin to understand why pacing is so important. If we are telling the truth, we can keep a steady pace. In police interviews, we often see suspects "stalling" for time, allowing them to construct a falsehood or cover story. Pay attention to the pace of a conversation and you will often sense when something "feels off." While this is something that is difficult to verbalize, it is something that can be felt. The truth of the matter is your years on earth have already made you an expert in this skill, which you use every day. Now is the time to pay attention to it and add it into your mentalist toolbox.

It is impossible for us to control every gesture and movement our bodies make. Often, by paying close attention, we can spot times when sight and sound seem to be fighting each other. This is an indication of falsehood. We see each side of the brain trying to keep the deception together, but in truth it is close to impossible to control these actions and have them work naturally unless we are telling the truth.

On *The Mentalist*, Patrick Jane is always very aware of the people around him. When he's interviewing a witness or a suspect, he's watching that person very closely—even when he may be pretending not to. If there's even a beat of hesitation or disingenuousness in a conversation, he picks up on it and exploits it throughout the rest of the investigation.

A faked emotional response is often easy to spot. A fake smile, for example, is often limited to movement just around the mouth. When someone smiles naturally, the whole face is involved: There's jaw and cheek movement, the eyes crinkle up, and the eyebrows push down slightly . This tends to apply to every emotion. If someone's expression of happiness, surprise, sorrow, or awe seems isolated to just one area of the face, that person is most likely faking it.

VERBAL CUES

Again, if a conversation doesn't feel natural, it probably isn't. Is the person giving you too many details, or maybe not enough?

Often a person who is lying will give very little attention to any details and give you a broad answer, expecting you to fill in the larger picture for yourself. Conversely, another verbal tell is filling in too many of the details. If the explanation becomes long-winded, it can mean that the subject is searching his or her brain for the best creative answer. Another stalling technique is the use of guttural noises or "ummm" to draw out the conversation and gain extra time to develop a story.

A change in tone is another giveaway that part of your subject's conversation is being fabricated. Less sophisticated liars will often just sound fake. They speak under their breath, jumble their words, and can be difficult to hear or understand. If only they would all make it this easy.

A good way to find out if someone is lying and to pick up on these verbal cues is to change the subject of the conversation quickly. Jane is always keeping suspects on their toes by throwing out non sequiturs. In the middle of a tense interview, he'll ask them where they bought their watch or compliment them on their home. A liar will follow along willingly and become more relaxed. A guilty person wants the subject changed; while an innocent person may be confused by the sudden change in topic and want to go back to the previous subject. When practicing this method, you'll find your interpretation of these indicators will be based in part on your prior experiences with the person and will largely be determined by how you "feel out" the interaction.

EASY TELLS

So here's what I want you to do. I've put together a cheat sheet on how to tell when someone is lying. You need to read the following information slowly and carefully. Actually, I suggest you read this section three times from start to finish. Allow the information to sink into your own mind.

Think of this overview as your best friend in getting started with lie detection.

- *Lip tells.* A puckering of the lips after a statement almost surely indicates a falsehood. Concentrate your focus on the area of the lips just under the nose. You will tend to notice a quickly forming attack of the arches of this region, which will allow you to assess the lie as the subject prepares to attack you with a pre-planned response. Looking effectively for this is great, but listening for it is even better. A person's tone will be enhanced before squealing out their retort.

- *Breathing tells.* When people get excited or charged, their breathing tends to get much deeper and faster as their pulse rate speeds up. Blood starts to rush, and they begin to perspire, while they stop salivating to deliver a fear response.

■ *Touching tells.* Look out for any facial touching. Touching of the face, ears, or neck is a useful tell. On the other hand, liars are unlikely to touch their chest or heart with an open hand.

■ *Tone and voice tells.* Is the person's voice aggressive, restrained, passive, or violent? Those could be some indicators, but telling if someone is lying from the tone of his or her voice actually can be quite difficult, if the person, well, has a lot of practice as a liar. After all, as they say, anyone can pass a lie detector if that person *believes* he or she is telling the truth. And so much of that comes through the tone of our voice.

■ *Rapid blinking.* When liars tell their falsehoods, they become excited, and when the excitement kicks in it creates rapid eye movement, which causes an increased rate in blinking. Eye squinting is a form of deception aimed at preventing the liar from allowing him- or herself to be seen by the investigator. FBI and CIA operatives detect this quite frequently. Subjects, knowing someone is hot on their trail and peering into their eyes deeply, begin to use a form of squint, which is thought to masquerade the tell.

■ *Covering one's mouth.* The first thing a liar will do is cover his or her mouth to ensure that secrets will not slip out. Can you remember the last time you did this? It's a subconscious sign that you know you basically cannot 100 percent trust yourself while under duress. Do this and you're basically giving yourself away.

■ *The tight-lipped mouth.* The teeth are clenched and the lips are pursed together, while there's also jaw tension, indicating stress and concern.

■ *Open lips.* It's a great tool to distract an astute observer. A liar opens the lips and darts his or her tongue out the side, so that the viewer stares at this and not at what he or she should be looking at.

■ *OMG mouth.* When someone's mouth is open wide enough for a fly to land in it, it obviously and blatantly indicates that the subject is in a state of semi-shock and cannot believe what he or she has just seen or heard.

■ *Folding the arms.* This is not necessarily a sign of a lie, but it could lead you to another one. It shows a resistance or a holding back, quite possibly of the truth.

Take a moment to allow this information to sink in and allow your mind to really understand the ideas and concepts that I am sharing with you. Take a deep breath in and fill your lungs with air. Allow yourself to become relaxed understanding that you have just enriched your own mind with techniques that will pay off tenfold the effort you have expended in learning them.

Remember you are already a master with these techniques, having used them subconsciously your entire life. Now is the time to pay attention to these skills.

The most important thing to remember is that you must not

generalize. Just because someone scratched an ear doesn't make that person a liar. The concept is to use all the methods while also utilizing your gut intuition.

Most lie detecting experts agree that a combination of body language, motor activity, and other cues must be used to make an educated guess on whether someone is telling the truth or a lie.

A REAL MENTALIST EXERCISE

Take a moment to visit www.youtube.com and search for footage of any recent celebrity scandals that might have occurred, specifically situations in which a person in the spotlight has told a lie. The classic examples I use when teaching are the recent "performance enhancing" drug cases in sports and the Bill Clinton "I did not have . . ." speech. Watch the body language of people we know were lying at the time. See if you can begin to spot common traits, such as touching the face, avoiding the heart/chest, never using an open hand to contact the body. These high-pressure situations often allow us to focus only on the nonverbal, innate communication that occurs. Often verbal communication at these times will be so well practiced that it is largely not worth our attention. However, due to the attention being paid to the verbal communication, we are offered real, honest nonverbal communication to help us work on our skills as a "human lie detector."

EYE-ACCESSING CUES

The eyes are, indeed, the window to the soul. The following information will allow us to better understand when and why people are trying to deceive us. Combining the lessons taught above with the following rules, we can begin to move toward knowing exactly what someone is thinking and when.

Ask someone a question and then watch the direction the person's eyes go. Whether the person glances up or down, to the left or to the right will tell you which part of the brain that individual is accessing and what his or her mind is processing.

The different directions of the eyes can tell you if a subject is trying to access visual or auditory information. Is the person remembering something, or creating a new image or sound in the mind?

These eye-accessing cues were developed as part of the theory of NLP, which is short for Neuro-Linguistic Programming. This approach was originated by mathematician Richard Bandler and linguist John Grinder in the 1970s. They were interested in seeing how behaviors and thoughts related to one another while we are communicating with others.

They discovered that the direction of your eye movement can be quite telling. See the illustration on the following page to see what they found.

So how do we put this great information into use? Let's take the following example.

Let's say Lisbon on *The Mentalist* is asking our prime suspect for an alibi. "Where were you on the night in question?" she asks.

• Up and to the left indicates that the person is trying to visually construct an image in their mind.

• Up and to the right indicates that they are accessing an image stored in their memory.

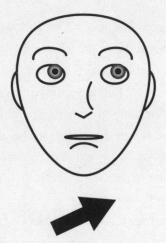

• To the middle and left represents auditory construction. They're trying to imagine what something would sound like.

• To the middle and right indicates that they are accessing a sound stored in their memory and that they've heard before.

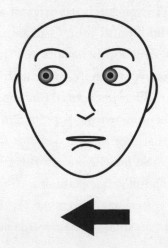

• Down and to the left represents them accessing a feeling, perhaps how they felt when an event occurred.

• Down and to the right represents them having an inner dialogue or chatter.

The bad guy replies, "I took a drive up to my cabin and spent the weekend fishing." As he answers, he looks to the left. This would indicate a made-up answer, as his eyes are showing that he's concocting a "constructed image or sound." If our suspect had looked to the right, that would have indicated a "remembered" voice or image, and thus Patrick Jane would have assumed that he was telling the truth. Clearly, though, our fisherman has something to hide.

Someone who looks up and then lowers his or her eyes, leaving them in that lower position for a majority of the time, is searching for closure or completion of the thought and that they are showing dominance in those areas.

But as with every other technique, this tool shouldn't be used as the sole judge of whether someone is telling the truth or lying.

A less risky use of the NLP system is as a tool to determine what type of person someone is. Since it relies less on generalizing about how any one person will react, it can often be a more accurate method. When I say what type of person, I mean is the person auditory, visual, or kinesthetic? Again, you can make this determination based in part on which direction a subject looks when he or she makes a statement or answers a question. You then use what you learn to establish a rapport with the person and play off his or her personality type, either to make the individual comfortable or uncomfortable.

- *Visual people (those who look up).* Visual people rely on the pictures in their head to make sense of the words they hear. They create pictures of concepts and will be very detailed in their responses because they're literally painting a picture in their minds.

- *Auditory people (those who keep their eyes level or in the middle).* An auditory person relies on the use of words. This person tends to make decisions based on how something sounds and if it's pleasing to his or her ear. An auditory person will say things like "that sounds great" and "I hear ya."

- *Kinesthetic people (those who look down).* Kinesthetic people focus their decisions on how something makes them feel. They tend to be emotional people who will make a decision about you very quickly.

Patrick Jane can be a charmer, based largely on his ability to identify whether a person is visual, auditory, or kinesthetic. He will tailor his conversation with someone based on this knowledge. Often he uses this talent to make his subjects feel comfortable, so that he's better able to catch them off guard when the time is right. Every now and then, however, he'll use his understanding of personalities to push all the right buttons and bring out the subject's hostile side. This can be just as telling and is only one of the ways that Patrick attacks the lies.

Attacking the Lies

So now that we have a pretty good idea of when someone is lying, what do we do with that information? Or more specifically, how do we attack the liar?

I don't mean physically attack the person. Let's not resort to violence here . . . Rather, how do we engage the liar verbally to achieve our goal, whether it's to have the person admit the lie, or simply to come around to our side of an argument or our point of view?

Attacking the liar doesn't always need to lead to an aha! moment when the person admits that he or she was lying and you get to proclaim: "I caught you!"

Rather, attacking the liar could mean simply that you get the person to retreat, allowing you to access the information that you need to access. An example of that could be an athlete accused of using steroids or another performance-enhancing drug. Perhaps your goal isn't to get the person to admit the steroid use, but instead you want to know who the drug was purchased from.

Maybe the athlete is refusing to admit use of the steroid,

which leaves you needing to break down that lie before you can find out who the supplier is. Is it critical that you lead this athlete to a huge epiphany and soul cleansing? No, you just want to knock the subject off his or her game long enough to get the information that you need.

But before we can do any of that, we need to know why people lie.

WHY LIE?

When someone lies to us, we have to question the motive or what the lie can do for that person. Whether it is a bold and blatant lie or something more subtle, a lie is an attempt to mislead or cover up the truth in order to protect a secret.

Everyone lies. Some people are malicious in their intent when they lie. Others say they only tell "white lies" so as not to hurt someone. But believe me, everyone lies.

We started lying when we were very young, maybe by the time we were three or four years old. When we're that young, our intent certainly isn't to be malicious; we aren't trying to get anyone in trouble. At three or four, we lie to try to manipulate our parents to get something as simple as another cookie, or we're simply trying to test our parents to see where our limits are.

In the episode "Throwing Fire" we learn that Patrick Jane became a master liar and manipulator at a young age. Raised as a "carnie," he first started using his talents to entertain crowds with his "psychic" abilities. Under the not-so-great influence of his despicable father, Patrick soon after went from showman to con man.

As we get older, we continue to see what power lying can have in our lives as a manipulative tool, and as some of us stray from higher moral standards, we use lying more and more. We begin to lie so much that we actually believe our own lies, which begs the question: If you believe your own lie, is it still a lie?

Well yes, of course it is. A lie is a lie.

WHAT'S THE TRUTH?

As you'll find with so many sections of this book, the most important thing to remember before using a mentalist tool is to get your own mind straight, but especially when dealing with a liar. It can be a struggle to not get lost in the liar's deception.

If you're going to try to rebut someone else's belief, then you have to have a pretty strong sense of your own convictions before you even start the conversation. But even more than that, you also have to know what the outcome of this conversation will look like. Is it the aha! moment, or is it simply dislodging the information that you need?

This concept of being prepared to deal with a liar is not that hard, and I call it the "behind belief." Just know what you want and be prepared to allow all of your questions and answers to come out of that belief and deep focus. This is basically your virtual life preserver. It's what you use to save yourself from the liar's constant deception.

So how do you prepare yourself?

Well the easiest way is to establish your belief and then list five things someone could do to try to change your mind or make you doubt yourself. List those five statements or actions and then go over in your mind how you would combat them. You're arming yourself with the tools you'll need in the worst case scenarios.

Don't be stubborn enough to think that there's nothing anyone could do to change your mind, because we all have our moments of weakness. So perform an honest assessment of the situation and prepare yourself in that way. Sometimes it can be helpful to try it out with a partner.

What if you don't have the benefit of going into a situation with time to prepare? Well then you simply have to solidify your belief on the fly. Take a second, and in your own mind just repeat to yourself that you know the truth and you can't be dislodged from your belief. You are a rock, and you hold all the cards.

INTERROGATION

So now that we know how to identify a liar and why a liar lies, how do we break the liar or get him or her to admit the truth? You'll basically need to employ a form of interrogation and do everything that you can to confuse the subject and otherwise throw the liar off his or her game.

Some of this might seem childish, and it probably is. Patrick's colleagues clearly think he's being immature at times. Cho once accused him of using his unconventional tactics out of a "childish need for drama." But at the end of the day, the whole team respects his uncanny abilities for catching criminals. His brand of childishness is on a grown-up level of thinking. Some of what you use to interrogate subjects will be meant to confuse them. Other times you'll want to try to gain their trust or simply have them become interested in what you're talking about.

Here are just some of the rules that Patrick Jane and all good mentalists follow to manipulate their way to the truth:

▪ *Don't be a threat.* Liars often lie because they feel threatened. So how do you combat that? Well don't come off as a threat. Make the subject feel comfortable and lull him or her into your confidence. If a person doesn't feel threatened by you, then he or she is more likely to open up, and then it's mission accomplished. In the third episode of Season 1 of *The Mentalist*, Jane stays on the beach—the scene of the crime—while his coworkers go back to the office to start on the case. He spends the day building sandcastles and playing chess with one of the beachcombers—a guy who just happens to be a person of interest in the case. Jane uses the camaraderie he built with the suspect to his advantage during questioning.

▪ *Offer help.* If you offer to help someone, that person will be more likely to help you. So figure out how you can assist a subject and he or she will warm up to you and lower the cloak of lies.

▪ *Flatter them.* I already suggested that you butter people up, and this is in the same vain. Many times in this book I'll tell you that flattery will get you everywhere. If you find something positive about the person and acknowledge it, your subject likely will become less antagonistic. Patrick Jane will sometimes flirt with suspects and witnesses to build this kind of rapport.

- *Common interest.* If you can find a common interest with your subject, you can help that person feel like you are genuinely interested in who he or she is, and the subject will be more likely to drop any guard that's up.

- *Ask questions.* Ask at least ten questions about the person. This isn't a game, but yet another way to make the person feel more comfortable with you and the situation.

- *Change the subject.* Not everything has to be about the lie. You can transition to a story or question that has nothing to do with the information that you're trying to extract. This will help you make the person feel more comfortable, and maybe even confuse the liar a little.

- *ABC: Always Be Closing.* That phrase is from the popular play and movie *Glengarry Glen Ross.* Basically, whichever of the tactics you use, make sure that you're always focused on and headed toward your goal, whatever that may be.

Armed with your knowledge of physical tells, verbal cues, eye-accessing cues, and effective methods of interrogation, you will become a human lie detector and, more importantly, a truth extractor.

CHAPTER FIVE

Controlling Your Audience

What is the ultimate objective of any mentalist?

It's mind control, isn't it?

Okay, maybe that sounds a little crazy, but it's actually quite a reasonable objective. I'm not talking about brainwashing a population in order to achieve world domination here. I'm not some kind of sci-fi movie villain. But it's true that just as we have the power to control what information people share with us, we also have the power to control the way other people think about us.

In controlling the way that people think about us, we can use all of the other tools we learn to build a powerful machine. That machine is the mentalist.

So let's dive into mind control for a bit, and then we'll bring it all back together to see how we use all of our tools to become a mentalist just like Patrick Jane.

Mind Control

So what is mind control?

I'm not talking about hypnosis or trances. We'll cover that later. Mind control is actually a very real thing that happens every day. It has happened to many of you reading this book and you had no idea.

As intimidating as it may sound, mind control is the act of systematically using manipulative methods to persuade someone to perform certain actions. If you look up the term on the Internet, you'll find synonymous terms like "brainwashing," "coercive persuasion," and "thought control." You'll frequently also find the term "unethical" used as part of the description.

The ethics issue arises so often because mind control frequently is associated with propaganda movements, Communism, and prisoners of war. When people think of mind control, cults and fringe religions immediately pop into their heads. They think of people being forced to perform unethical acts against their will.

In teaching you certain aspects of mind control, I hope you choose to use these skills as morally as possible. Perhaps you've purchased this book with a hope of becoming a professional mentalist. Or maybe you're an officer of the law and are hoping to use Patrick Jane–like techniques in the field.

If, however, you're a businessperson looking to gain an edge in the boardroom, this brings us dangerously close to that line that separates good from bad, ethical from unethical. So I ask that you seriously consider your motives when employing these techniques. After all, you never know when someone might start using these skills against you.

Make no mistake that these *are* skills. You're exerting your will over someone, sometimes for an extended period of time and other times in a very short time frame. For instance, you might simply be doing a favor for someone just so you can hold it over that person at a later time. Or maybe you're purposefully being introverted and quiet so that people always will wonder what you're thinking and what you're up to. Or maybe you're simply exerting your power over someone through confidence and strong will.

So let's explore what exactly that power means.

Power

For many of us, power is the ability to get things done—our way.

Sometimes it's a direct order that we give, sometimes a suggestion we make, or a request of a favor; but the result (if you have power) is always that the other person acts and you derive a benefit from those actions.

Even those who don't have the powers of mind control are still trying to achieve this sort of power. They are trying to manipulate the people and situations around them to their benefit. They want the chips to fall their way and are willing to do almost anything to achieve that. They might not be strong enough mentally to accomplish this goal, but make no mistake that it is indeed their desire.

EVERYDAY POWER PLAYS

This manipulation of people happens at work, on the playing field, and even in our families. You come across this every day, even if you don't realize it. Consider that person who always comes to you asking for advice. In one respect you might chalk that up to the person trusting in you and wanting to seek out your opinion. On the other hand, non-leaders often want to seek out others for guidance, and they will be attracted to powerful, strong leaders. You may already have more power than you realize.

Power really is so critical to who we are and what we're trying to achieve in life. The people who have it will do anything to maintain it. And those who don't will work as hard as they can to attain it. That's why I'm dedicating such a large section of this chapter to the simple idea of power and how you achieve it, how you take on a powerful persona.

You have power over your employees because you pay their salaries. If you are an expert in a special field, it's because you know the best way to handle matters. In a legal dispute, power is derived from having the law on your side, or from having enough money to hire the best lawyers. When it comes to lifestyle and the way we live, power often stems from money. The ability to pay for things by whipping out a credit card exudes a sense of authority.

In politics, the major players derive their power from the ability to influence a vote or action. They either influence the politician by holding something over his or her head, or they influence the constituent by saying this politician will bring you something if you vote for him or her.

And then there's the power that derives from being talented, charming, and capable; from being up-to-the-minute and knowledgeable, so people know if they let you handle things for them or listen to your advice, they'll come out ahead.

COMPETING FOR POWER

If the world were fair and equal, one would have no need for the upper hand, for the advantage, for power. But of course the world isn't fair, which often means that in a competitive situation you can't expect to be given the same opportunity as your competitor. You can't expect that you'll both start from the same place and be granted the same opportunities, because it doesn't happen like that. Some of us are more gifted than others. Others of us are afforded the finest education, coaches, clothes, and food, while others get by on the scraps. The haves and have-nots will follow us all of our lives. So how do you overcome?

You must keep your eyes and ears, and indeed all of your faculties, open for any clue or other tips that will move the balance of power in your favor.

Whenever possible, make sure you get more than an equal chance.

Ever hear the expression "follow the leader"? It's a fact that people either will lead or follow. Leaders are generally thought of as "winners." Doesn't everybody want to be a winner?

Keeping Up Appearances

Patrick Jane is no slob. He's always meticulously dressed and appears calm, cool, and collected. He knows that to be a leader, you have to dress like one. Haven't you ever heard the advice: "Dress for the job you want, not the job you have." It's all about the impressions you make.

THE RIGHT LOOK

You need to look the part and act the part. That includes exuding confidence and appearing to be someone powerful. If an individual comes up to you wearing a stained, ripped shirt with torn jeans and mismatched shoes, are you going to take that person seriously? Are you going to buy into that person enough to allow him or her to influence what you eat for lunch, let alone allow that person to control your mind? Probably not.

People indeed are impressed by how someone looks. They often are not aware of why they treat one person like a VIP and another doesn't even get a second glance. Their reactions may be subliminal, below their conscious awareness. But take it from me, if you're well dressed, neatly groomed, hair trimmed, etc., and you're driving a snazzy car, you'll be well received; while a guy who's wearing sloppy clothes, appears unshaven and unclean, and drives an old heap will hardly get any attention at all.

Here's the thing: In this field, money and power beget money and power. So you can't wait for your ship to come in before you buy that first nice suit or get something other than that jalopy. Your ship never will come in as a mentalist if you're wearing that torn shirt.

If you're short on cash, get out the credit card and buy yourself a decent suit. Consider it an investment in your career and that will help you attract work and money. If your car leaves a cloud of black smoke in its wake and the muffler can be heard from miles away, consider renting a car for the occasions when you're trying to make an impression. Rental cars don't cost that much and driving a good one pays dividends in the power sphere.

Try to join clubs and organizations (business, social, political) that have important and influential members. If at first you can't become a member, then maneuver a member into taking you as his guest.

The more the world thinks you have, the more you'll get. Those who belong to the power elite are those who *appear* to belong to it. Unless he's a highly recognizable celebrity, even a millionaire will be turned away from a classy restaurant if he's not well dressed.

ACT THE PART

There's another extremely important factor in appearing power-ful, and that is in your manner of doing things.

You must move, speak, and act from power.

Have you ever met the grandson of a man who amassed a fortune, and wondered how a man who did so much could have a grandson who seems like such a weakling?

It's true; that grandson could never have gotten rich based on his own merits. If he hadn't inherited his family's money, he'd be poor, because he's weak and incompetent. And it shows.

People who, like yourself (remember flattery gets you every-where), are capable of making money now are people who can act in a strong style that almost seems to draw money like a magnet.

Language and the way you speak can say as much as the ideas that you're trying to relay. Equally important, however, is your body language and the way that you stand, walk, move, sit, the gestures you make. In fact, some scientists theorize that more than 50 percent of the way we interpret messages from people is delivered through their body language. Just consider the body language of others and how it influences your perception of them. What does your body language say about you?

Consider the business man dressed in a sharp suit, who stands quite upright and tall, offers a strong handshake, and is quick to insert his opinions, even before he's asked.

Now it would be easy to compare that image to a waiter or

dishwasher at a low-class restaurant who is passive and clearly disappointed and dissatisfied with his work. Clearly that's not someone we'd be likely to take suggestions from, whether we come by that decision consciously or subconsciously.

But what about another businessman who's wearing the exact same expensive suit as businessman number one? But unlike our first businessman, this gentleman walks around with a slouch, offers a wet noodle as a handshake, and only speaks when spoken to. Is this someone we'd likely allow to influence us in any way? I doubt it.

And how about Patrick Jane, how does he act?

Isn't he always quick to offer his unsolicited opinion? He's often standing almost uncomfortably too close to people, and in doing so asserting a sort of power over them and keeping them on edge without even saying a word. He's often interjecting his opinion, even when it's not necessarily wanted.

He oozes assertiveness. That's how he uses body language to his benefit. But his behavior isn't all just superficial. There's more going on beneath the surface, so that his power moves are convincing.

Self-Control

Few things fluster Patrick Jane. Or at least that's what he'd like everyone to believe. In truth, through all of his years in entertainment, Patrick has become quite a good actor. He keeps a carefully orchestrated façade in place at all times.

As viewers of the show, we have more opportunities to see what's under this front that he puts up for all of the other characters on the show. So we know that the only things that can really make him lose his cool are Red John—the man who brutally murdered Jane's family—and the memories of the family he's lost.

When Patrick fears that a woman he's dated, Kristina Frye, may have attracted the attentions of Red John, we really see him sweat for the first time. His even temper falls by the wayside, and he argues with the woman for leaving herself vulnerable and not taking the threat seriously. In anger, he lets go of his better judgment and storms off, even though he'd originally planned to stay and protect her. As a result, Kristina disappears, presumably at the hands of Red John.

By losing control of himself and his emotions, Patrick loses control of the situation.

The consequences aren't always so dire, but it's actually quite common for things to go south when we lose our focus. I, for instance, need to set aside all of my personal issues, emotions, and worries when I perform in front of an audience. If the audience starts to see me stressing about a routine or feeling insecure about my performance, then I've already lost them.

So before taking control of the audience, I need to take control of myself.

Be Confident

The meditation techniques that you learned in Chapter 1 will take you a long way toward controlling your stress levels. That said, you can do hours and hours of "oms" and it will still feel a bit unnerving to stand in front of an auditorium of hundreds of people. Your hands may want to shake, your voice may want to crack, but you have to take a deep breath and remember that you own that room.

GAIN EXPERIENCE

As with so many other skills, practice really does make perfect. Few things will boost your confidence like knowledge and experience. Over time, you start to learn most of the possible scenarios that could crop up during a reading.

Let's face it. That's what usually makes us nervous. The unknown. What if my subject doesn't cooperate? What if I lose my train of thought? What if my reading is way off base?

I'll talk a little bit more at the end of this chapter about how to handle the unexpected. You'll never be able to anticipate every possible chain of events. Instead, the more experience you gain, the more comfortable you'll become with handling any situation that comes your way.

Obviously, practice and preparedness are key to feeling in control of your performance, but to create the same cool exterior that Patrick Jane exudes, you might consider bringing a celebrity with you.

CELEBRITY MIRRORING

Now, I know most of you reading this book don't know a celebrity, and can't afford to hire one. I'm talking more about channeling your inner celebrity and bringing that persona into a situation with you.

We all have a celebrity that we consider the definition of "cool." We all want to be that cool too. Celebrities have an ability to make people feel comfortable with them. It's something they were born with and then worked on to perfect their crafts. It's the reason they're paid millions of dollars to be on the big screen. People see them and want to be them, want to believe them.

So to become a successful mentalist it wouldn't hurt to take on some of the personality traits of your favorite celebrity, assuming the celebrity is the calm, cool, collected, magnetic type. Richard Simmons, for instance, might not be the best example to use for this particular exercise.

Start by taking the time to study some of the unique aspects of the celebrity that you've chosen. How does this person speak, walk, sit? What's the celebrity's posture like? Does this person speak with his or her hands? Look people straight in the eye?

Now imagine that you're stepping into the shoes of this celebrity, or if you feel more comfortable with it, imagine that the celebrity is stepping inside of you, pulling your strings. This isn't to say that you're about to become a professional impersonator of this celebrity. If you've chosen Sean Connery as your celebrity and people start to ask why you're suddenly speaking with a Scottish accent, then you've taken this way too far.

So now how do you use this celebrity to control your audience?

Well it's all built on a premise that people like people who like themselves and are confident. People are drawn to confidence. So if you take on the traits of a confident celebrity, then you will be more confident in yourself and your own talents.

Use that confidence to charm the socks off the person you're trying to read. You might not actually feel the confidence at first, but if you start by pretending, you'll eventually start feeling as strong as you appear.

MAKE A MENTALIST NOTE

The perfect opportunities for studying celebrities and their demeanors are awards shows. You'll get a lot of insight into the way celebrities talk and move by watching the red carpet interviews before the Oscars, Emmys, and Grammys. Choose the celebrity you decide to mirror carefully. It's important to discern which ones seem confident and comfortable in their own skin, but don't appear overly aloof. Too much arrogance can turn off a crowd just as easily as insecurity.

HAVE FUN

You've probably noted that Patrick Jane smiles *a lot*. Unless Red John is in the picture, Jane keeps his mood light and never takes himself or the CBI's investigations too seriously. This is cause for some contempt from Lisbon at times, but in truth, it's part of what makes him so good at what he does.

As an entertainer, I try to remind myself and my audience that all of my performances are in good fun. Let's face it, I have a really fun job! When I smile and laugh and make jokes, I'm putting myself and everyone around me at ease.

If everyone is having a good time, the audience is much more receptive and I feel good about what I'm accomplishing.

So lighten up!

Keep Everyone Else Off-Balance

Even if you're not feeling your best, or you're having an "off" night, you can still come out on top by keeping your subject off-balance. If you become really good at this, then other people won't even know you're besting them. This is the secret of all great illusionists.

DIVERSION AND MISDIRECTION

There are times when diversion and misdirection can be a mentalist's best friend. I'm thinking about a form of misdirection a little more advanced than "look at my thumb" or "your shoe is untied," but in reality it's not that much different.

Why might we need to utilize this tool of misdirection?

Well it's actually quite simple. If people aren't focused on you and what you're doing, they're less likely to see you employing one of your mentalist tricks and more likely to slip up and let their own guard down.

How would a magician use misdirection? Well an easy example is to call someone, possibly an attractive woman, up to the stage to assist with a trick instead of going out to the crowd to bring the trick to the woman.

The key would be to get to the part of the trick where the magician would have to perform something sneaky, and then call the woman to the stage. It's fair to say that the eyes of an overwhelming majority of the audience will be focused on the woman walking up to the stage, and not the magician, leaving the magician free to do whatever he needs to do, whether that is to slip something into his pocket or to mess with a deck of cards.

So that's how a magician would use diversion or misdirection, but how about a mentalist?

Well misdirection isn't as complex as you think. It's really anything that you can do to throw people off their game, or to be a bit more scientific, it's anything you can do to get people to stop focusing on the outside world and instead focus their attention inward. Not sure what that means?

Well typically when you meet someone for the first time you'll offer some kind of greeting, like a nod or handshake. The person with whom you're meeting also will nod or shake your hand in return while they observe who you are and what you're about, trying to come up with an initial observation about you. So they are focused on you and the outside world.

But what if instead of offering a traditional handshake you offer an extremely strong handshake, or you hold on to their hand for a second longer than you normally would, or you offer a very weak handshake? Basically, what if you just do something out of the ordinary?

Then suddenly the person with whom you're meeting will begin to focus his or her attention inward and contemplate what that handshake meant. An outside observer would think that the person is part of the meeting/conversation just as anyone else would be, but in reality this person is preoccupied with this question of why you shook hands like that. With that, you've diverted the person's attention and have taken control of the situation.

It's almost too easy, right?

Misdirection can stem from more than physical actions. Consider what you say along with how and when you say it as potential forms of misdirection.

Stringing several large words and complex sentences together can misdirect people and completely throw them off their thought and potentially off any argument that they were attempting to make. Also consider answering a question with a question.

For example, if a salesman asks, "Do you want the extended warranty for this television?" you respond with "How many colors does this television come in?"

It's a simple, harmless question. But it isn't the response the salesman was expecting, which could allow you the opportunity to take control of the situation and extract the information you really need, such as "Do I really need the extended warranty?"

So far this discussion of verbal misdirection has been rather hypothetical and based mostly on the idea that you want to take people out of their comfort zones.

But there is a way to handle a conversation or line of questioning that constantly places the focus back on your subject and, more importantly, takes it away from you. This is called Socratic Questioning, and it's basically a method of answering questions and statements with more questions.

SOCRATIC QUESTIONING

Socratic Questioning is derived from the more common practice of the Socratic Method.

The Socratic Method, of course named after Socrates, basically is a form or method of debate between two people who are on different sides of an argument or belief. The method's intent is to stimulate discussion and critical thinking in order to arrive at some commonality.

This form of debate is a back-and-forth of asking and answering questions at a brisk pace that ultimately will promote critical thinking and potentially lead to one of the parties contradicting himself, strengthening the other party's argument.

The questions are used to test the logic of a belief or statement. The subjects go back and forth, continuously asking and answering questions in an attempt to validate their own beliefs. This system also is referred to as a *negative* method of hypothesis elimination. Essentially the subjects partaking in the exercise eliminate false hypotheses by finding errors through their questioning, ultimately drawing closer to a better hypothesis.

The Socratic Questioning begins with one party responding to an initial question as though it were an answer. The original questioner then is forced to come up with a new question, and so the process of critical thinking continues.

Socratic Questioning truly is critical thinking at its finest. It is based on the belief that a simple, surface-level answer is not enough. Instead, it encourages people to go deeper to get to the root level of an issue or belief. A or B? OK, so you chose B, but why did you choose B?

That's what Socratic Questioning is all about, making you take another look at your beliefs in order to debunk what's false and ultimately land on what is true.

So how do you do it?

Well who better to ask than the Foundation of Critical Thinking, a nonprofic educational organization with more than three decades of research and study, which states that people engaging in Socratic Questioning should consider the following:

- Respond to all answers with questions that force the respondent to develop his or her thinking in a deeper way.

- Try to understand why people believe what they do and then follow the implications of that belief through to further questions.

- Treat all beliefs as though they will connect to further thoughts and beliefs.

- Consider that all thoughts and beliefs are in need of further development.

- Recognize that any belief does not exist on its own but rather is connected to a network of other thoughts and beliefs. You need to be able to recognize that network and ask questions based on it.

While considering the bullet points above, there are other actions you can take to prepare for a session of Socratic Questioning.

The most effective way to prepare is to consider the end goal and then backtrack from there. So you need to establish what the final question you want answered is, and then from there establish the network of questions that you believe will need to be answered in order to reach that final goal.

For instance, the Foundation of Critical Thinking suggests

that if your ultimate goal is to land on an answer to the question "What is multiculturalism?" you first will need to be able to settle the questions of "What is culture?" "What is the basis of culture?" and "What are the factors about a person which determine what culture he/she belongs to?"

What Questions Should You Ask?

Well the questions you ask obviously will be dependent on what questioning or issue you're ultimately trying to resolve.

But David Straker, a former consultant with Hewlett Packard and author of the book *Changing Minds: in Detail*, suggests there are some tried-and-true questions that you can begin with as you start to explore Socratic Questioning. The questions fall under the five classifications of "Conceptual Clarification," "Probing Assumptions," "Probing Rationale," "Questioning Viewpoints," and "Probing Implications."

Here are some sample questions under each of those headers:

- Conceptual Clarification
  Why are you saying that?
  What exactly does this mean?
  How does this relate to what we have been talking about?
  What is the nature of . . . ?

- Probing Assumptions
  What else could we assume?
  You seem to be assuming . . . ?

How did you choose those assumptions?

Please explain why/how . . . ?

■ Probing Rationale

Why is that happening?

How do you know this?

Show me . . . ?

Can you give me an example of that?

What do you think causes . . . ?

■ Questioning Viewpoints

Another way of looking at this is . . . , does this seem reasonable?

What alternative ways of looking at this are there?

Why is . . . necessary?

Who benefits from this?

■ Probing Implications

Then what would happen?

What are the consequences of that assumption?

How could . . . be used to . . . ?

What are the implications of . . . ?

Again, the questions you ask very much depend on what you're trying to answer or accomplish. So it's important that you understand that ultimate goal and then backtrack from there.

Who Uses Socratic Questioning?

As I said, the method is based on the critical thinking teachings of Socrates. Socrates indeed was a teacher at heart, and so this method still is used by teachers today. But it's also used in any venue where it's believed debate can help lead to resolution of an issue over a belief.

The method also is used by professional trainers and those who work in human resources. The practice can help achieve a desired outcome for an employee or help correct a poor attitude toward the business or the job. Through open questions and dialogue, the lead party can direct the conversation and help achieve the stated goal while also leaving the perception of an open conversation that is dependent on the responses of the subject. This way the subject does not feel threatened.

Additionally, the Socratic Questioning method is very common among psychotherapists, who often use it to resolve disagreements among family members.

As mentalists, we want to use this method both to distract our subject and to extract as much information as possible. We can use this tool to obtain control of a verbal encounter, which could take the form of a debate, negotiation, or sale. As a mentalist, you're always trying to assert your power over a situation.

MENTAL MIND TRICKS

This book isn't intended to teach you magic tricks, but there are some mental mind tricks that I can teach you that can help you in your effort to take control of whatever situation you're in. Some of these tricks can serve as ice-breakers, while others have more practical uses.

For instance, what if you can get people to turn around and look at you without tapping them on the shoulder or saying a word to them? Would that be useful as a mentalist? Certainly! You can take control of your subject with just a gaze.

So how do you accomplish this? Well you have to stare at the person intently. Not for minutes at a time, but rather thirty to forty seconds tops. Most of the time you want to stare at the top of the person's spine, but different people have different locations on their bodies that serve as this control center.

The secret here is that you want to look through the person, so if you're staring at the top of the spine, you want to imagine you're looking through to the chest and face. I know it sounds silly, but try it. Stare at the exterior of the skin on the back of the neck and picture that skin getting hot. Then see it hotter and hotter, until it starts to glow orange in your imagination. I promise you that you will get that person's attention. When the person does turn around, respond with your smiling eyes and then actually smile back, and your subject will be transfixed by you and curious about who you are and what you're all about. You will automatically have a certain amount of control over that person.

If you think about it, this is something you've probably already had some experience with. Haven't we all had the feeling that someone's staring at us? Sometimes the hair on the back of your neck will rise and you'll turn around quickly to see that someone's been watching you. How could you have known? It's like having eyes in the back of your head!

Some would say that this is a psychic phenomenon. Rupert Sheldrake, for example, is an English biochemist who has done some controversial research on parapsychology. He published a paper called "The Sense of Being Stared At" which supports the idea that our vision gives off a kind of energy. He believes that just as a magnet has a surrounding field, our "minds likewise extend beyond brains through fields." The person we're starting at, therefore, can feel this "perceptual field."

Others have a more practical explanation. Perhaps you're being picked up in the person's peripheral vision. Maybe one of the person's other senses is picking up on your presence. Could a change in your breathing pattern have tipped your subject off? When you're concentrating so intently, you're probably quieter and more still. Maybe your subject just picked up on this change in the environment.

Whatever the case, I think you'll find this trick surprisingly effective.

Another way to gain someone's full attention is through touch. Touching the wrist of someone with whom you're shaking hands can create a powerful response. When you meet someone and shake their hand, take the index finger of your left hand and quickly and gently touch their wrist, just for a split second.

The late Milton Erickson took this a step further and developed the hypnotic handshake induction. Erickson was a psychiatrist and the founding president of the American Society for Clinical Hypnosis. He used unexpected touches during a handshake to put someone into a trance that he would later reinforce with other hypnotic suggestions.

I don't take this technique that far. But by executing the handshake in a way that my subject finds surprising, I'm throwing him or her off guard and gaining the "upper hand," so to speak. Also, humans crave sensory experiences by nature. So by touching a sensitive area of skin, I'm satisfying some of those natural desires and gaining a certain amount of gratitude.

One important note is that if you get caught or questioned for either staring or touching the wrist, just shake your head and say you're "out of it" or some excuse like that. Most people won't question it.

MIRRORING

We've already talked about mirroring a celebrity to create confidence, but there's another kind of mirroring you can use to gain control of the person you're talking to. Instead of taking on the mannerisms of someone you've researched, you copy the person with whom you're conversing. You've probably practiced a type of mirroring in your day-to-day life and didn't even realize it. Often after spending a lot of time with someone, we tend to pick up that person's mannerisms, speech patterns, expressions, or even the person's accents. Often a New Englander will come home with a Southern accent after visiting Savannah for a few days. Usually it's completely unintentional, a kind of psychological quirk. But if you learn to mirror at opportune times, it can be a powerful mentalist tool.

Essentially, the practice of mirroring will cause a person to like you. It comes from the world of Neuro-Linguistic Programming, and in its most basic form you begin by the subtle act of copying the actions a person is taking. After a short time you will find that this person will begin to become "in synch" with you. Through this mirroring you're building up an instant rapport.

How do you develop this rapport and synchronization? Well first remember that you can't be obvious. I'm not talking about a game of Copy Cat here, where you simply repeat every action that someone is making in front of you and reiterate everything that that person says.

Instead, you want to be a bit more subtle. For instance, try to observe the person's breathing pattern and mimic that. Is the person breathing fast or slow? Are they deep or short breaths? Recognize the pattern and mimic it.

How about key words that the person uses? A lot of people overuse words such as "like" ("That's like so cool that you can, like, do that!") or stall with "ummmm" or "and uhhh." Try to identify some of these habits and repeat them back to them as naturally as you can.

Same goes for body language. Does the person speak with his or her hands? Does the person pace when speaking or stand in one spot? Observe your subject's movements while he or she is speaking and then find a way to incorporate the same actions when you're conversing back. If you become too obvious, the jig is up. The person will immediately be suspicious . . . and well, kind of freaked out.

So why mirror someone? Because once you are in synch with a person, you can begin to lead that person's actions. Your subject will subconsciously start mirroring you back. This becomes a powerful tool for an astute mentalist, as it allows you to lead movement and in the process reveal some useful information.

For example, let's imagine you wish to view both sides of a person's hands. In order to accomplish this you might first start by simply striking up a conversation with the individual. If you hear that the person uses a word over and over, then you'll start to use that same word. While you're talking to the person, observe his or her breathing and do your best to mimic it. If the person gestures toward his or her head with the left hand, wait a second then do the same with your right hand (that is if you're facing the person). Continue this for a couple of minutes, and soon you'll start to see that you're indeed in synch with your subject. So when you're ready, naturally take your hands and with your own movements cue the other person to turn his or her hands, and see what happens. You might be pleasantly surprised.

Don't doubt the power of the mirroring technique. In fact, professionals in the customer service industry often are trained on mirroring. Why? Customer service isn't the easiest of jobs. Often you're faced with an upset client seeking some sort of refund or for an issue to be resolved. And "upset" is probably understating it.

A professional with some training should be able to mirror a customer, in turn taking control of the situation and alleviating the tension. The customer service job becomes a lot easier and the client's attitude about the company and the particular issue likely will improve dramatically. That's not to say a refund still won't be necessary, but it's more likely that the customer will leave happy.

SUBLIMINAL MESSAGING

Chances are you really don't know how easy it is to control what someone standing in front of you thinks.

The person can be someone of power and leadership, someone who's very successful at his or her profession. Still, with some very easy tricks you can control what that person thinks and impress that individual immensely.

Here's a fun way that Patrick Jane does this in Episode 9 of Season 1 ("Flame Red").

At the beginning of the episode Jane tells Lisbon that he can read her mind. He asks her to imagine a shape inside of another shape and project that image into his mind. Jane declares that she was thinking of a triangle within a circle. After initially denying that Jane guessed correctly, Lisbon concedes that he's indeed correct.

How did he do it?

Well, there are two things at play here. First of all, the way Jane words his command narrows down Lisbon's potential answers. Jane asks her to imagine a simple shape "like a square, but not a square." So right off the bat we've eliminated one of the three most popular shapes someone would imagine, with the other two being a circle and a triangle.

Always remember that by narrowing down your potential answers you're taking control of the reading and improving the odds that you'll hit on accurate information.

The other thing that Jane does is casually use his hands to form the shapes that Lisbon ends up guessing. When asking her to imagine the first shape, Jane holds his hand widely apart but in the form of a triangle. When he asks here to imagine the second shape he basically uses both hands to make a circle. He doesn't make it as obvious as using one finger to draw a circle in the air the way a four-year-old would. Instead he uses his hands the way anyone might when making a statement during a conversation.

Both actions, with the triangle and with the circle, are subtle, but they're definitely there. And they certainly impact Lisbon's answers.

There's a popular mentalist by the name of Derren Brown who is very well known for his ability to get people to think what he wants them to think. In one instance he sits someone down and asks him to think about the perfect birthday gift. If this person could have anything in the world for his birthday, what would it be?

After some thought the gentleman answers "a BMX bike," and of course that's what Derren Brown just happens to have wrapped in a box behind him.

So how did he do it?

Well if you search for this video, which has been viewed

thousands of times online, you'll see that this trick was accomplished through subliminal messaging. Subliminal messages are used by performers and even advertisers to make someone comfortable with a product or idea through quick uses of certain words or images.

Research disputes whether the technique truly is effective in advertising, but it clearly is effective in this Derren Brown routine. Throughout his sit-down with this man, Brown repeatedly uses and accentuates the letters B-M-X in the conversation.

One sentence even is as blatant as "I want X. Like a really nice car like a BM or an Xbox." Additionally, Brown is tapping the man on the shoulder each time he says B-M-X; locking it into the man's psyche.

The man is so entranced by Brown that he doesn't even notice that sentences like "A really nice car like a BM or an Xbox" make no sense. The room is also decorated in shapes that are reminiscent of a bike; connected circles that look like the tires, for instance. And while the subliminal messaging may seem obvious to us on the outside looking in, it's anything but obvious to the person sitting there.

So am I telling you that subliminal messaging works every time? No, certainly not. But this routine does teach us a few things. First of all the action of locking in positive reinforcement with a touch is very important and can be used in a number of different routines. The way you use this effectively is to initiate the tap when your subject agrees with you on a statement or answers a question with a positive response. So if you're sitting across from someone and you ask, "You're feeling pretty good today, aren't you?" and the person responds with a yes, then give him or her a tap.

Continue this throughout the first couple of minutes in response to positive statements, but then after that only give the tap when the person agrees to something you want them to agree to.

So what you've essentially done is created a signal for positive responses, and you are now using it to dictate what is and isn't a positive response. You're essentially making up the person's mind for him or her, and you're also locking in ideas that your subject should remember or, rather, that should sink into his or her subconscious. So every time Brown taps his subject along with saying B-M-X, the B-M-X is being received as a positive statement and something that rests in a positive location in the subject's subconscious.

As for continuing to hide B-M-X within the conversation, that's simply repetition, and repetition is something that always will help guide someone in a certain direction as long as it's done without being overly obvious.

These tactics are not for the novice mentalist and take significant training, but they can be effective.

Escape Plans

As I mentioned before, it's impossible to predict when something will go wrong. There are times when outside circumstances may cause our control to slip, but there's always a way to get it back.

No matter what happens, it's imperative to remember that a mentalist is never wrong. If a reading goes off course a bit, that's just part of the mentalist's journey to better understanding. There may be bumps along the way, but they're only dead ends if the mentalist stops and let's them *be* dead ends. Instead, the mentalist simply keeps going until he or she reaches that place of understanding.

If, however, a subject is uncooperative, just move on. You're offering a remarkable form of entertainment that's based on cooperation, connection, and communication. You're already attempting the impossible with these tricks, so if someone wants to make the process even more difficult, let that individual find someone else to fight with. The experience of mentalism is a gift for the spectator. If someone rejects that gift, find a more appreciative recipient.

There have been very few circumstances that I wasn't prepared for, because I practice diligently and educate myself as much as possible. I've learned how to roll with the punches. In fact, one time when I was performing at MIT in Boston, my luggage was lost on the way there. In those suitcases I had props and tools that were part of my act, and they were now nowhere to be found. With only two or three hours to pull together a forty-five-minute show for about a thousand people, I went on a shopping trip to the local office supply store. I bought everything I needed to amaze the audience. In the end, I never told them I'd lost my luggage, and I received two standing ovations. Sometimes you just need to get creative.

Another time I performed at a party in New Jersey and the

power went out. I pulled out my emergency flashlight, my client lit some candles, and the result was rather magical. Sometimes the unexpected can actually make for a better show!

Harnessing Your Power

Strong impressions, Socratic Questioning, and subliminal messaging can be truly effective tools for exerting power. It's up to you to decide how and when these techniques could be best used to your advantage, but what if you took your control of others one step further.

What if you could erase most of their inhibitions? We'll talk about that next.

CHAPTER SIX

Hypnotism

Every now and then the CBI agents come across a nut that's particularly tough to crack. Sometimes witnesses just won't talk, usually out of some kind of fear. Maybe they're afraid of incriminating themselves or maybe they're worried they could become the next victim.

Lisbon and Cho take the interrogation as far as it will go, but if they don't have enough evidence to hold the person, they sometimes have to throw their hands up in the air. It's impossible to force someone to talk, right?

Maybe not.

In the episode "Red Hair and Silver Tape," when the team can't get the victim's best friend to admit what she is hiding, Patrick Jane sneaks in after the interview and plants a hypnotic suggestion to make her talk the next time he sees her. At first, it doesn't seem as if the trance worked, but sure enough she spills her guts the next time she's at CBI headquarters.

Hypnosis is a frequently misunderstood state of mind. I'm going to try and clear up some common misconceptions while trying to explain to you the true nature of hypnosis and how it can be utilized.

First of all let me tell you that hypnosis is commonly misunderstood because of the film and stage hypnotists who have popularized the craft. You know the types of spectacles I'm talking about. Embarrassing portrayals in movies sometimes have the hypnotist inducing the subject to bark like a dog. Then the hypnotist forgets to undo the suggestion, leaving the person to bark like a dog for the rest of his or her life.

That's not what hypnosis really is. Someone under the influence of hypnosis isn't a slave to the person doing the hypnotizing. The subject is still operating under free will. And while the popular representation of hypnotism portrays it as putting someone into a semi-sleep, the reality is that it actually makes the person hyper-attentive.

In fact, hypnosis is an altered state of mind and consciousness that everyone, including animals, experience on a daily basis. Surprised? Hypnotism isn't something just for carnivals and magicians.

Let me tell you in no uncertain terms that hypnosis is in fact a real thing. It's concentration; plain and simple.

You might not know it, but you are hypnotized when you are sitting entranced watching a movie or when you are driving and go three exits past the one you were supposed to get off on. You might not believe it, but that time when you were mowing the lawn and were focused on nothing but the straight lines you were creating with your lawnmower, you were hypnotized too.

So What Is Hypnosis?

In its most simple terms, hypnosis is a process by which someone accesses another person's subconscious. As we perform daily tasks, we're making use of our conscious mind. From the second the alarm goes off in the morning until we fall asleep on our pillow at night, we're making conscious decisions throughout the day. You consciously address the issues you're presented with. You problem-solve and consciously choose what words to say.

But while you're consciously acting, it's subconscious decisions that actually lead to the action taking place. It's our subconscious, a pool of memories, feelings, and desires, that we draw from when we decide whether to utter a word or turn left or right.

That hunch you had isn't just a hunch, it's your subconscious. That idea that seemed to come from nowhere, well your subconscious had already seen that idea through to fruition before you realized you had thought of it.

Your subconscious also takes care of all of the autopilot-type stuff that we never think of. You know, like breathing. You never think about breathing, or blinking, or anything like that. It's your subconscious that handles those things for you. And how about when you're driving a car? Are you consciously checking that mirror every five to ten seconds or is that your subconscious acting for you?

OK, so you're saying to yourself, "I understand conscious and subconscious, but what does that have to do with hypnotism?"

Well hypnotism is basically the act of putting your conscious mind to rest and allowing your subconscious to have free rein. It's achieving a sleeplike mental state while you're still awake.

So what happens when you subdue your conscious mind? Well you're accessing a section of your brain that is less inhibitive, which is why people under hypnosis won't necessarily go against their morals (which I'll get to in just a minute) but may be a little more playful and, well, bark like a dog.

So let's talk a bit about who first discovered this phenomenon.

HOW IT ALL STARTED

Seventy years before the term "hypnotism" was coined in 1842, German physician Franz Anton Mesmer was practicing a technique that put his patients into a trance. He had observed a clergyman's exorcism of a "lost soul" and noted the subject's altered state of consciousness. Mesmer didn't believe in demonic possession, but he developed his own medical theories after doing further research. He proposed that we humans have a mysterious magnetic fluid in our bodies that needs to be balanced and free-flowing in order to maintain good health. When he passed his hands over patients' bodies while they were in these sleeplike states—he called them "crises"—he thought that he was unclogging that fluid and "healing" them. While he often had impressive results, Mesmer was discredited and largely dismissed by his peers and the overall medical community.

Years later, another physician, James Braid, became interested in what was by then called mesmerism and applied his own science to the phenomenon. His work is largely responsible for validating the use of these trances in the psychiatric community. While Braid didn't believe in some of the more magical claims of the "magnetists" of his day, he couldn't argue that the entranced were certainly experiencing an altered state of consciousness. He studied the mysterious process further and explored the different ways it could be therapeutic to patients. Because of this work, he's regarded by many as the very first hypnotherapist.

The trance, at its most basic form, was induced by placing hands on the shoulders of the patient and stroking the arms downward. Additionally gentle passes were made with the hand and at times a sort of patting of the forehead.

Hypnosis has come a long way since then, but some of its uses haven't veered all that far in the last 150 years.

WHY HYPNOSIS?

It's important to be clear on the difference between mentalism and hypnosis. As a "mentalist" you are reading the body language, words, and any other outward actions of a person. You are reading the signals that a person gives off and translating those signals into a clear picture of who that person is, which lets you influence his or her behavior to some extent.

On the other hand, having someone under hypnosis allows you the opportunity to exert a bit more control over that person. It allows you to lull the person into a state of being that leaves him or her highly suggestible.

Under hypnosis, another person will act in a way that you choose. So while mentalism can be considered more observational, hypnotism is closer to being the puppet master.

Hypnosis is the highest level of concentration and focus of the mind, and in addition to entertainment, it can be used as a more practical tool, to aid relaxation or to achieve pain relief.

For example, hypnosis can be used to alleviate pain both before and after surgeries. In a study by the Mount Sinai School of Medicine in New York, one hundred women underwent hypnosis for fifteen minutes before breast cancer surgery. Another one hundred were given fifteen minutes of psychological counseling instead. While the women had been under the trance, the hypnotists had set the patients' expectations for reduced pain. The researchers found that the women who underwent hypnosis needed less anesthesia, reported having less pain, and were in surgery for less time than the other group. The medical usage of hypnotism isn't a new phenomenon. In fact, the mesmerism technique was used to control pain during amputations in India more than 150 years ago.

But how do we combine hypnotism with mentalism if we're ultimately trying to get something out of someone or to read them?

Well through hypnosis you have access to people's emotional core. You can learn about how they truly feel, not just how their conscious mind is allowing them to feel. Often when you ask people a question, their conscious mind will not allow them to answer honestly. They make the conscious decision not to tell you that they're angry, happy, or sad.

But with access to the subconscious, there are no smoke screens, there is no politically correct answer. The subconscious mind will spout the truth when asked. It will provide true emotions and the memories connected to those emotions. However, as the person in control of the hypnosis, you also potentially have the ability to plant false emotions or memories within a subject's subconscious. Pretty powerful stuff, huh? More on that in a bit.

POPULAR FEARS

One of the biggest misunderstandings is that some people think they can manipulate everything that a person does if they've gotten that person under hypnosis. In reality, a person under hypnosis will not violate his or her moral or ethical code or compromise his or her values any more or less than if the person were not hypnotized.

Another fear that people have is that if hypnotized they will never wake up. In reality, if you hypnotize someone and simply walk away, they eventually will wake up on their own, just as if they had simply fallen asleep.

While we don't want people to be fearful of hypnotism, I'll be honest with you . . . People who do have a certain amount of fear are easier to hypnotize. If they fear hypnotism, that means they believe in it and are already more likely to be entranced than someone who has been skeptical about hypnotism for decades. Fear and skepticism are very different emotions.

So now that we know the true meaning of hypnosis and its potential uses, and have debunked some of the fears about it, let's move on to the hypnotizing.

Lulling Them into Hypnosis

Hypnosis begins with the induction.

When you perform hypnosis, you try to clear your subject's mind of all other thoughts and sounds except those that emanate from yourself.

There are many ways to induce hypnosis. One of the most common is using phrases that we've all heard on a television show or in a movie:

- "You're getting sleepier and sleepier."

- "You are getting more and more relaxed."

- "Your eyes are getting heavier and heavier."

- "You're deeper and deeper in sleep."

As you utter one, all, or some combination of these phrases, your voice should become deeper and softer as you progress. Imagine that you're lulling a baby to sleep. In this case the "baby" is the subject's conscious mind.

Independent research will uncover numerous induction techniques if you decide you want to take the time to become a master at hypnosis. Some of these techniques are basic, while others are fairly controversial. And while I'll outline a few, what they all have in common is that the person performing the hypnosis should have control of the concentrated focus of the subject at all times.

Focus is key. You need to control the subject's focus, and you need to provide a relaxing outlet that will help the subject reach the hypnotic state that will lull the individual's conscious mind to sleep.

Creating imagery in the subject's mind is often used in induction techniques and can even be used for self-hypnosis. The most common form of this imagery is that of descending, whether it is down steps or down a mountain or hill. With each step in the gradual process of descending, the subject is coaxed (through your voice) deeper and deeper into the trance. I will offer a sort of script for this sort of hypnotism later in this chapter. This technique isn't uncommon, and any of us who have practiced yoga are familiar with the almost trance-like state that is achieved as you imagine your body truly being pushed through the floor, with all of your energy being released.

The combination of using a deep, soothing voice with the visualization of descending is called *progressive relaxation and imagery*, but that's not the only way to lull someone into a hypnotic state.

OTHER TECHNIQUES

The *fixed-gaze induction* or *eye fixation* is what we're used to seeing in the movies and on television. If you can't remember fixed-eye induction, then just call this one the pocket watch induction.

In this scenario you're having someone focus his or her sense of vision so intently on one object that the person is ignoring everything else that's going on, visually and with the subject's other senses. While the progressive relaxation and imagery technique involved having subjects focus on your voice and the images being created in their head, this technique has them focus on your pocket watch—or another object you employ for the same purpose. As subjects' focus on the watch begins to heighten, you begin to speak to them in that deep, soft voice.

While this method was quite popular in the past, it's not used as regularly today and is said not to be as successful as other methods. Perhaps that's because people can't get over the fact that they've seen this on television or in a movie, which blocks their conscious mind from being able to rest.

The *rapid induction* process is based on the hypnotist's ability to overload someone's mind with sudden and firm commands. These commands may not even be verbal, as another common name for this type of induction is the *handshake induction*. Shaking hands is something that comes naturally to us, but at the same time we're programmed to believe that a handshake should go a certain way, follow a certain social code. So when someone switches up part of this interaction, we're caught off guard and are more susceptible to hypnotic induction. This technique is very complex and really shouldn't be attempted without instruction from a professional. It also should not be practiced on someone without that person's knowledge, as it could get uncomfortable for both parties very quickly. I'll just leave this technique at that and allow you to research it some more on your own.

Finally there's the *loss of balance* technique, which incorporates the rocking portion of lulling a baby to sleep. I already stated that you should talk to your subject as a parent would when trying to lull a child to sleep. This technique incorporates the physical portion of that process by using slow, rhythmic rocking, which throws off the subject's equilibrium and primes him or her for hypnosis.

Beyond these induction techniques, there are other ways a person can reach this state. As I mentioned, we go in and out of trances throughout the day without being subjected to any of these practices.

For instance, in Season 1, Episode 5 of *The Mentalist* ("Redwood"), Jane jostles the mind of a suspect/victim by driving her along the same stretch of road where a crime occurred. He also plays the same music that the woman and her friend were listening to on the night of the crime and prods her to remember what happened, filling in the gaps for her at the same time.

Jane may not have used a pocket watch or a handshake induction, but make no mistake, this woman was indeed in a trance when this occurred, and she was reliving the events of that night. It's just another powerful and dramatic example of hypnotism.

WILLING PATIENTS

The amount of time it will take to hypnotize someone is largely dependent on that person's willingness and cooperation. Many people will be looking for a way out of their conscious minds and will gladly glom onto your commands and calming persona. Others will be much more reticent and will be tougher to crack. With that said, it could take only a few minutes to hypnotize someone.

No matter who the person is, you shouldn't simply jump into the hypnosis. Instead, ask a few questions that will give you a good idea of how receptive the person will be. Ask the person to imagine floating through the air and see what the person does. Ask the person to release all of the energy from his or her arms and gauge the person's reaction. You've already become skilled in the art of detecting lies, so you should be able to tell if your subject is sincere or just going through the motions.

This advice is offered in the context of you performing hypnosis as a sort of act or with friends. Obviously, in *The Mentalist*, Jane isn't always afforded the opportunity to judge whether the person he's dealing with will be a willing participant. Nevertheless, he's able to tailor his induction technique to the individual subject and the situation at hand. That's something that can take years and years of practice.

They're Hypnotized, Now What?

So now that you've got them in this trance, what do you do with them?

Remember, you can't have them go out and knock off your enemies or throw eggs at the IRS. First of all, it's not responsible on your part, and secondly, people won't ignore their moral compass just because they've been hypnotized.

For example, in Episode 18 of Season 1 of *The Mentalist* ("Russet Potatoes"), the CBI team searches for someone who uses hypnotism to get people to do his dirty work. Over the course of the episode Agent Rigsby, a partner of Patrick Jane's, is hypnotized himself. While hypnotized, Rigsby slams a suspect's head into a table during an interrogation of him.

"I thought you couldn't hypnotize somebody against his moral character?" questions another member of the CBI, in regard to Rigsby's outburst.

"Rigsby has a brutal streak," Jane replies. "If you didn't know, now you know. It's not an uncommon trait in those who choose to go into police work."

So while hypnotism can't force us to do something against our morals or beliefs, it may make us more likely to act on beliefs or traits that we generally keep hidden.

"Deeply hypnotized subjects are very suggestible and have very little inhibition," Jane continues.

Jane then has Rigsby close his eyes and asks him to imagine what he most wants to be doing at that very moment. He has

Rigsby open his eyes and then tells him to carry out that action. Rigsby walks over and kisses a fellow agent.

Jane didn't have Rigsby do anything that he didn't want to do, deep down. There are, of course, limitations. But with all of that being said, hypnosis does give you some power by putting the conscious mind to sleep and allowing the subconscious to come out and play, just as it does when we're all fast asleep in our beds.

As I stated earlier, this power of hypnosis can be used to help alleviate pain or, as we've seen time and time again on television, help people quit nasty vices like smoking and biting their nails.

Take weight loss, for instance, and how the conscious and subconscious battle when we're deciding whether or not to eat that third piece of pizza or cut another slice of pie. We know that our conscious mind ultimately is making the decision to eat, but what in our subconscious is influencing that decision? Is it past disappointments that have left us seeking food as a comfort? What if under hypnosis you were reprogrammed to no longer associate food with comfort? Would that help you lose weight? I suspect it would.

■ ■

MENTALIST FACT
Hypnosis and Smoking

In 1992 researchers from the University of Iowa culled the results of more than six hundred studies that took into consideration the experiences of more than seventy-two thousand smokers. The location of the subjects who were looking to stop the habit reached from America to Scandinavia and other parts of Europe.

The researchers found that hypnosis was the most effective treatment. It was three times more effective than the nicotine patch and fifteen times more effective than the smoker relying on his or her own willpower.

■ ■

POST-HYPNOTIC SUGGESTION

In order to help a client achieve weight loss, the hypnotist might plant a post-hypnotic suggestion in the person's mind to feel less tempted the next time the person sees a piece of cake.

Post-hypnotic suggestions are rather like reminders that the hypnotist programs into the subject's mind to feel a certain way or behave in a certain manner when faced with a specific circumstance after awakening from the trance.

Let's go back to the "Red Hair and Silver Tape" episode, in which Jane hypnotizes a young woman to be a more cooperative witness. During that session, Jane uses an imagery induction technique. He tells the woman to think of him while she is falling asleep that night and to imagine that she can feel completely weightless. She can "fly away and leave all burdens and worries and fears behind." Then Jane taps her and feeds her a post-hypnotic suggestion. He tells her that the next time he says hello to her, she'll tell the truth, because it will give her that same feeling of serenity. While not exactly an approved method of police work, his hypnosis trick gets the job done and the witness comes forward.

In this instance, Jane merely plants an emotional suggestion. He wants to instill a feeling of peace in the woman the next time he sees her, so that she won't be ruled by her fear. He gives her the tool she needs to tell the truth.

Other times a hypnotist might plant a suggestion for the subject to act a certain way, instead. This brings us back to that example of making someone bark like a dog. Perhaps for the act, the audience member is hypnotized to bark every time he hears his name, even after he's finished on stage and is back in his seat.

In hypnotherapy, post-hypnotic suggestion can be used in a number of ways. Maybe a therapist will plant a feeling of confidence every time his rather demure client sees her boss. One of the most common post-hypnotic suggestions is actually used to make the hypnosis process easier the next time around. The subject is programmed to feel calm and serene the next time the induction process begins.

But in the instance of this book we're discussing hypnosis as it pertains to mentalism and Patrick Jane. While Jane has crossed the line a few times, they certainly aren't too fond of the idea of using post-hypnotic suggestion down at police headquarters. It's not one of the more subtle—or legal, for that matter—approaches.

Instead the type of hypnosis that Patrick Jane uses on a more regular basis is conversational hypnosis.

BECOMING A JEDI

Most of us remember the scenes from the *Star Wars* movies when a Jedi changes someone's mind simply through tone of voice. The Jedi is confronted and simply changes the confronter's mind by saying the opposite thing.

So is it really that easy? Can you change someone's mind simply by contradicting what that person has said? Not likely, unless the other person is extremely simpleminded.

But that's not to say conversational hypnosis isn't a real thing and doesn't in some instances resemble the tools used by those fictional Jedi.

In reality, conversational hypnosis is a series of choreographed steps that you will use to manipulate someone's views so that they more closely resemble what you're trying to achieve.

The idea of conversational hypnosis was first introduced by controversial psychotherapist Milton Erickson. As I've addressed earlier, Erickson believed that hypnotic trances weren't occasions that come along once in a blue moon and have to be induced by someone else. Instead, Erickson believed that these trances happen to people several times a day, every day, whether it's when you're focused on a computer screen for long periods of time or waiting for a bus and focused on nothing but the newspaper being held eight inches from your face.

Erickson thought that conversational hypnosis could circumvent any resistance from people who were not so cooperative.

Instead of conflict, he chose to develop a rapport with the person, while using indirect suggestion and confusion to induce a trance.

How do we do that?

RAPPORT

Developing a rapport with someone for the purpose of hypnosis isn't that much different from the conversational patterns I addressed earlier in the book when it came to detecting lies.

You want the person to feel comfortable with you and you want to establish a calm and trusting environment. How do you do that?

Well the quickest and easiest way to achieve that goal is to simply agree with whatever the person says. If the person declares that the weather is terrible, then you echo that belief. If the person thinks a situation is a positive or negative one, then you tell the person that you share that opinion.

You're bringing the person into your trust and also lulling his or her conscious mind to rest, because the person is not having to consider rebutting you when you're agreeing at every turn.

Don't forget about the mirroring techniques that we covered in Chapter 5 as a way of establishing rapport. If you have the time to mirror your subject, and lull him or her into a sense of calm and security, you can move on to the next step of hypnosis.

CONFUSION

After you've developed your rapport with the subject, you next want to confuse the person. The easiest way to do that is to ask a quick question that will leave your subject befuddled. So if the person says that a situation is hopeless, then you can suggest that the very next person who walks down the street could be the answer to your subject's problems, or you can take a more confrontational or resistant approach by stating that you know the situation is hopeless and can't imagine how this person thought he or she could achieve this goal or how anyone could expect to reach it.

After just a minute the person with whom you're speaking may be so confused that he or she will very suddenly take a much more optimistic approach and you'll hear something like "Things aren't so bad. We can do this."

Another way to gain control of the situation is to use a form of double-talk that I learned and developed with the Fantastic Fig, a celebrity attorney turned professional magician. The trick is simply to say "scateramus harsbar." That's right, I said scateramus harsbar.

No, the words, if you can call them that, don't hide any secret meaning among the community of mentalists. What they really are is a way to control someone by short-circuiting that person's thought process.

You go up to someone and say the magic words—or

gibberish—in the context of an otherwise normal sentence or conversation. For instance, something like:

"Scateramus harsbar," you shout at someone.

"What?" they reply as they approach you.

"Scateramus harsbar, did you?" you follow up with, in a lower voice. Or you could try "Didn't we meet at Scateramus HarsBar?"

With that simple back-and-forth you've now likely got your subject coming in closer to you, trying to understand what you're saying and what you're about. Your subject is trying to figure you out, and while doing that he or she can't take the time to watch everything else you're doing. So if you choose to wow the subject with a couple of the mentalist tricks that you've learned, it should be a little easier because you've already got the person off balance.

SUGGESTION

Finally, if the tide hasn't changed on its own, this is where you insert your suggestion during the conversational hypnosis.

So through confusion and redirection you may have gotten someone to go from thinking a situation is dire to actually having them say, "Wait, I can do this." Now you can follow that up by saying, "You feel better about the situation now, don't you?"

It's likely the person you're speaking with will offer a positive response to your question.

So those are the basics of conversational hypnosis. If it seems easy, it's not. It takes experience on a number of levels. You have to practice your ability to meet someone on that person's level or to agree with that person no matter what. It's not as easy as you think. You then must practice the questions that you'd ask to throw someone off of his or her game or confuse someone. How would you confront someone's statement by saying the complete opposite? You have to think quickly.

Triggers

An important aspect of hypnosis that I haven't addressed yet is triggers.

A trigger statement or action could be the way you get someone into a hypnotic state or jostle someone from one.

It could be a key word that you associate with relaxation or inhibition while the person is in a suggestive state, or it could be as simple as a slap on the arm, which will jostle someone from a trance.

Both examples have been used on *The Mentalist*.

For instance, in the episode we already discussed where Agent Rigsby is hypnotized, Jane is asked to free Rigsby from the hypnosis. Jane says he can't release Rigsby from the hypnosis because he isn't the one who hypnotized him and he doesn't know the trigger word.

"It'd be like you and me playing Marco Polo in the Atlantic," Jane says of trying to figure out the trigger word.

But hypnotism doesn't always have to be that elaborate. In another episode Jane hypnotizes a suspect quickly and easily through the use of a lighter and his calm voice. When he's ready to release him from the trance, he simply slaps him twice on the arm, and the man comes to.

The type of trigger you use to bring someone out of a trance can depend on the person who's been hypnotized and how deeply he or she has "gone under."

Self-Hypnosis

Finally, I'd like to share with you some techniques for self-hypnosis. The process of putting yourself under hypnosis really isn't that much different from putting someone else in a trance.

Just like when you hypnotize someone else, you'll need to start by lulling yourself into a trance. You'll use the same practices that you would otherwise and clear your mind of everything other than a specific spot on the wall or an object swaying in front of you. You'll chant a simple "om," count backward from one hundred, or imagine that you're gradually going down a long set of steps. As you descend these steps, you'll feel yourself becoming calmer and more relaxed and slipping deeper and deeper into a trance state.

Getting yourself to reach this state is not a simple task, and as with everything else it requires practice. But in the same way that you guide another person in a trance, you'll be able to begin to suggest things to your own subconscious. Having established a list of affirmations and previously prepared statements, you can begin to repeat those to yourself, installing them into your subconscious. This will help you affirm your actions and build your self-confidence.

All you really need to be able to achieve self-hypnosis is a quiet room and the time to dedicate to it. Once you've finished the hypnosis, you begin to picture yourself ascending from the trance state and suggest to yourself that you will wake up refreshed and energized.

▪ ▪

SCRIPT FOR HYPNOTISM

You can use the following script when hypnotizing one or more subjects. You can even use it as a guide for self-hypnosis.

Please take a piece of paper and a pen or pencil and focus on a desire.

Write the desire down. For instance something like "In the next thirty days I will . . ."

Don't be too general and simply write something like "I will be skinnier." Instead of simply jotting down "I want to lose some weight," write "By the end of the next thirty days I am going to weigh 149 pounds," or whatever the goal may be.

Now consider the how and why of your objective.

How are you going to accomplish it and why must it be done?

This is not designed for you to lose consciousness and develop amnesia, so don't be afraid.

As a matter of fact I would like you now to do some moderate stretching exercises and then be seated. Begin by taking a deep breath in and then closing your eyes. By listening to the sound of my voice, I want you to go even deeper now and release your breath. Good. Now take another deep breath in and while keeping your eyes closed hold the breath, and now slowly release it. You are going to start to notice that you will feel a little bit tired . . . and sleepy . . . You will start to feel quite relaxed . . . Take another deep breath in . . . and breathe out.

Good. Now slowly open your eyes. Without moving your head, I want you to continue to listen to the sound of my voice and stare at a small spot on the wall. Just stay transfixed and focus on that point please as you breathe in . . . and out.

You soon will begin to notice that your eyes are getting sleepy and are starting to water and your eyelids are now becoming heavier and heavier.

Just keep your eyes fixed in that position and begin to notice that your head is now getting heavier and heavier as you breathe in again. Breathe in deeper and keep focusing on the point on the wall.

Your eyes are really, really tired and you want to close them but you can't. It's OK to allow them to begin to flutter. Yes, your eyelids are fluttering, but they are just so heavy. You are getting deeper and deeper into a relaxed state, and just letting your eyes close now would be so peaceful and relaxing.

I am now going to count backward down from ten to one, and with each number that I count down, you will find yourself more and more relaxed.

10. You are now getting sleepier and sleepier.
9. With each number I count down, you feel your body starting to get sleepier and heavier. When I reach the number one, you will allow your eyelids to drop and close your eyes.
8. Continue to relax and notice that your body is starting to feel heavier and heavier and your head is beginning to tilt from its weight.
7. Your eyes are fluttering even more . . . blinking, trying to stay open and awake—and you allow yourself to sleep.
6. Getting closer and closer to one, you start to really let the feeling of your head and body go. You are no longer there, you are just floating effortlessly in your mind.
5. Take another deep breath in and sink down deeper in the chair and imagine that every inch, every pound of you is getting absorbed by the chair.
4. You are safe here and will be closing your eyes very soon. I actually notice your eyes closing now. Just melt away into the chair and allow all your stress to melt with you.
3. You're closing your eyes now.
2. You're deeper and deeper into relaxation.
1. And now close your eyes and breathe.

Start to see a light in your mind's eye and watch this orange light as it gets closer and closer to you.

Its warmth is very healing and nurturing. Feel it getting closer and closer to your body and making you become warmer and warmer. Just begin to block out any external noises that you hear and stay in your chair, happy, content, and limp like taffy.

You have now completed the basic induction and can insert suggestibility tests and other suggestions into a person's subconscious.

Moving on to waking the client up

I am now going to count from one to ten, and when I reach the number ten, you will feel alive and awake and more refreshed than ever before.

1. Start to feel more alive and awake.
2. Feel your eyes moving around and your eyelids becoming unstuck.
3. Breathe deeply as you are ascending on an escalator.
4. You are coming higher and higher on the escalator.
5. Start to open your eyes.
6. You're going to feel amazing . . . and happy.
7. You're starting to wake up now—you are starting to feel a lightness around your body . . . lighter and lighter, more and more awake.
8. You're starting to come back now and opening your eyes.
9. You're coming back and
10. Now open your eyes slowly and welcome back.

■ ■

Once you've performed hypnosis on your own, you might develop your own script—a method that works best for you. It's all about trial and error.

Now let's get out of our subject's head and get to the staple of every mentalist: reading people. I think you'll be surprised how much you can find out about a person without having to unlock their subconscious.

CHAPTER SEVEN

Readings

People are fascinated by what they can't explain, which is why they gravitate toward palm readers, psychics, and television celebrities who seemingly are able to converse with the dead.

So these people we encounter at fairs and watch in the movies and on television, are they telepathic? Can they perform feats of extrasensory perception (ESP)?

Of course not!

More likely they're mentalists who are using the techniques of hot and cold reading to make you believe that they have a connection to another spiritual plane.

This chapter will reveal some of the secrets behind "otherworldly" sources of information and show you how you can perform almost-instant feats of magic and mentalism.

Otherworldly?

Before we can debunk the feats of "telepathy" and "ESP," we first must know what the people who perform them are claiming to be able to achieve. We can come across these showmen at any state fair or on any street corner in a major metro area. But those aren't the only places we can encounter these "skills."

They can be found in comic books, popular television shows (of both the fictional and "reality" genres), and in some of our most famous literature.

Claims of someone being able to perform telepathy or feats of ESP are so common that police departments are still seeking out mediums, much as Kristina Frye was called into an investigation on *The Mentalist*.

But what these detectives are getting aren't people who can speak to the other world. Instead they're really getting their own Patrick Jane.

I Want My ESP

From grade school to the athletic field the term ESP is one that's thrown around pretty loosely, but what does it mean?

When a basketball player makes a no-look pass, we might hear an announcer proclaim, "He has eyes in the back of his head. He must have ESP." Same goes for hockey.

And what about when someone finishes your sentence for you, or spits out a thought before you can? Is that ESP?

Well the technical definition of ESP is the ability to receive information, not through the traditional physical senses, but through the mind. You may have heard it referred to as a "sixth sense."

ESP is the umbrella term for a number of other so-called psychic abilities, including telepathy and clairvoyance. If someone tells you he or she did something on a hunch or because of a gut instinct, the person is actually claiming to have a sixth sense that guided him or her to act in that way. The person might be unaware of claiming to be the holder of an extrasensory ability, but that's exactly the case.

A popular example of ESP can be found in the movie *Ghostbusters* when one of the scientists holds a card with a shape on it and asks the person being studied—and with numerous sensors on his head—to concentrate and try to identify the shape on the card. Every time he guesses incorrectly, the patient receives a shock.

The cards being used in that scene are called Zener cards, named after their designer, Karl Zener.

Zener designed the cards, which include shapes like stars, circles, and wavy lines, in the early 1930s as a way for him and his colleague, J. B. Rhine, to conduct experiments in extrasensory perception.

During the experiment one person is the "sender" and the other is the "receiver." The sender must focus on the image with

hopes that the receiver will pick up on the thoughts that the sender is trying to send across the table.

There are five shapes in a set of Zener cards, so a receiver has a 20 percent chance of guessing the correct shape. A rate of success above 20 percent would suggest some semblance of an extrasensory skill, or just that the person is very lucky.

Rhine claimed to have found several subjects who scored much higher than that 20 percent after many, many trials. He believed that these individuals had a "gift." Critics at the time thought that Rhine was being duped by some of his subjects, who were actually cheating during the testing.

Today, various studies claim different levels of skepticism among scientists when it comes to these paranormal abilities. But the most reputable studies show that an overwhelming number of scientists—more than 90 percent—are highly skeptical of these people and claims.

So how do they do it? How does a receiver read a sender?

The Big Secret

So I'll now teach you the big secret of how you can pretend that you're some sort of paranormal. You'll impress your friends, scare your enemies, and confuse your coworkers.

The two ways people pretend to know you and everything about you are hot and cold readings.

Hot readings are when a mentalist uses knowledge learned about you, typically gathered by staffers before your onstage meeting, that the mentalist uses to "read" you. Hot readings are common among television psychics and faith healers. They generally have more time to prepare before meeting with a subject.

The other technique is called a cold reading.

Cold readings are much more complex for performers or "psychics," because they're going in without any pre-gathered information about you. They're going in cold, hence the term. But by the end of the performance you'll feel that they've known you your entire life.

NO MAGICAL POWERS

Before I get into cold readings I feel that I have to make it clear that I am not a psychic, and I have *no interest whatsoever* in providing anyone with a psychic reading! I do not read tarot cards, palms, astrological charts, or any other "paranormal" paraphernalia.

I do make use of cold reading as a supporting technique within my formal performances of mentalism. It can increase the personal impact of a routine by introducing personal information about an audience member that I couldn't possibly have known in advance, having never met this person before.

This chapter does not provide a method for performing psychic readings or a technique to talk to the dead. This chapter is not aimed at providing you with material to convince the world that you have supernatural powers.

On the other hand, I do want to provide you with a powerful and tested technique that will add impact to professional mentalist routines and performances. This chapter will provide you with shortcuts and tips to ensure you do not repeat the same mistakes I did when I began including cold reading techniques within my performances.

So my approach to cold reading is from the stance of a professional performer. I include it in my formal performances as an additional layer of deception. If you begin with a routine that is already strong and surefire, the addition of cold reading methods can tip it over the edge into new and exciting uncharted waters.

I always combine cold reading techniques with the *leading reading* approach (more on that later) to ensure I am many steps ahead of my audience long before they are even aware the reading has begun.

OK, so let's now dive into cold readings.

Cold Readings

Cold reading is not really a "trick" in the way a magician might think of a trick. Rather it is a set of methods, techniques, and concepts that allow the performer/cold reader to gather secret information about a spectator that is then used to project the illusion of psychic ability.

These techniques use the performer's keen sense of observation, which allows the mentalist to form an initial impression of the spectator, skills I've already addressed.

This first impression then will allow the performer to move forward with statements that open the reading based on a fundamental understanding of human commonalities and psychology.

Something like "You badly cut your right knee as a child." Of course you did. Who didn't?

When you have developed some confidence with cold reading, you soon will surprise and amaze even yourself with the impact it can add to a formal or casual performance.

SETTING IT UP

You need to have a sense of purpose when beginning your readings and to determine what it is that you are trying to provide for the subject.

You need to study the individual intently, but do not let the subject see the kind of real focus you are using. It is often helpful to have music, candles, an assistant, or other distractions going on while you are beginning your work with a subject. Study the subject's dress, shoes, way of speech, stance, dialect, and tattoos.

What does the person's makeup and perfume tell you? What is the person trying to hide. Is there some kind of cover-up? Is the subject overdoing it?

What does the person's jewelry tell you? What does the subject want the jewelry to tell you?

These are clearly just starting points for you to build into real solid readings as you weave in and out of all the techniques covered in this book. Remember each tool is designed to work seamlessly with the others.

You will need to master all aspects of reading people in order to appear to know someone's story from the cradle to the grave.

HOW COLD READINGS WORK

What leaves people susceptible to cold readings?

Well among the mentalist community we all refer to it as the "Forer Effect," named after psychologist Bertram Forer, or "Barnum Statements," of course named after P. T. Barnum.

Barnum Statements are ones that appear personal but in reality apply to many, many people. As I said earlier, "You badly scratched your right knee."

Or how about these:

- ▪ "You're having issues with a relative."

- ▪ "You have several boxes of old photos in your house."

- ▪ "You're sometimes insecure."

Did any of those statements resonate with you? Of course they did.

Through the use of these statements the performer seeks to elicit responses that will open the door to other feelings and issues the person being read may have. It could be that the person reacts with happiness or sorrow. Or perhaps the person just blurts out additional information, like "You're right, my dad and I aren't getting along!"

So why does this work? Well that's where the Forer Effect comes in.

It's long been found that people are eager to make connections between what someone says and their own lives. You know what I'm talking about. We all know one person who takes this to the extreme. That person who, whatever we're talking about, always has to relate the topic of conversation to his or her own life and say, "Oh my god that also happened to me."

So when a reading is occurring, people have an innate desire to find a connection with what is being said. And if they can't immediately find one, they'll look for different interpretations of the statement until they do, then ignore the fact that it took them so long to make the connection.

Forer found this to be true in the most interesting of ways.

WHAT'S YOUR PERSONALITY?

In 1948, Bertram Forer administered a personality test to a group of students. After the test, he told them that they'd each be receiving a unique personality profile based on the test, and he wanted them to grade the profile by giving it a number from zero to five. A grade of zero would mean that the profile was way off, while a five would mean that it was dead-on.

After the grades were received, Bertram announced that the average grade was a 4.26, meaning that in general the students felt that the profiles were very close to providing an accurate picture of who they were. What they didn't know was that each student had been given exactly the same profile, and this is how it read:

> Some of your aspirations tend to be pretty unrealistic. At times, you are extroverted, affable, sociable, while at other times you are introverted, wary and reserved. You have found it unwise to be too frank in revealing yourself to others. You pride yourself on being an independent thinker and do not accept others' opinions without satisfactory proof. You prefer a certain amount of change and variety, and become dissatisfied when hemmed in by restrictions and limitations. At times you have serious doubts as to whether you have made the right decision or done the right thing. Disciplined and controlled on the outside, you tend to be worrisome and insecure on the inside. Your sexual adjustment has presented some problems for you. While you have some personality weaknesses, you are

generally able to compensate for them. You have a great deal of unused capacity that you have not turned to your advantage. You have a tendency to be critical of yourself. You have a strong need for other people to like you and for them to admire you.

Forer is said to have gathered the elements of this statement from various horoscopes. The statement was later used by the famed P. T. Barnum, who is believed to have been the author of the famous statement, "There's a sucker born every minute."

Indeed a sucker is born every minute, which makes knowledge of this cold reading skill and Barnum Statements so important. In truth, all people arc far more gullible than they would like to believe.

While this is an interesting fact and an important thing to sit and ponder for a moment, it also provides a wonderful manner in which to demonstrate the nature of cold reading to those who may be led to believe they've been read through more supernatural means. When the "psychic" was supposedly communicating with the dead or predicting their future, was he or she employing the Forer Effect on them?

Indeed in the past few years we have seen the likes of Derren Brown, James Randi, Penn & Teller, and many others make use of this very technique in skeptical demonstrations. If you doubt the power of Forer's original all-purpose reading, print a few copies of it, hand them to your friends, and ask each of them to score how effective you were in summing up his or her personality. I think you will be shocked at the overwhelmingly positive reactions you will receive.

SELF-DECEPTION

I've already shown you how easy it can be to deceive people based on mentalists' ability to use percentages in their favor. If we know most people believe they're strong leaders, then using that statement as part of a cold reading is a no-brainer.

So we've established that many people think of themselves in ways common to them all. And we've established that we can use that to our advantage. But we're missing something, aren't we?

Ah yes, self-deception. Just because 70 percent of people see themselves as good leaders, that doesn't really mean they're all good leaders, does it? Of course it doesn't.

These people have duped themselves into believing what they want to believe, which in essence is self-deception. They're justifying false beliefs about themselves.

What we need to understand as mentalists is that almost everyone suffers from this self-deception in one way or another.

This concept was described very well by Justin Kruger and David Dunning, a pair of Cornell University psychologists, when they stated the following:

"People tend to hold overly favorable views of their abilities in many social and intellectual domains. This overestimation occurs, in part, because people who are unskilled in these domains suffer a dual burden: Not only do these people reach erroneous conclusions and make unfortunate choices, but their incompetence robs them of the metacognitive ability to realize it."

So now we understand the key phrases we can use to make people think that we "know them," and we understand that these people are often willing to receive these statements with open minds because of this concept of self-deception.

So now how do we put all of this to use?

FLATTERY IS EVERYTHING

"You're a generally well-liked person."

How many people would disagree if that statement was made about them? Even those people who generally are not well liked still perceive themselves to be quite popular.

Essentially positive statements go a long way toward greasing the wheels of a cold reading. That might seem like a no-brainer statement, but additional studies performed after Forer's research was completed show that the more a reading is infused with positive statements the more a person will be receptive toward that reading.

Additionally, the person being read wants to feel important and unique. If the subject feels that this reading is about him or her and no one else, the subject will try to connect with it, going down deep into his or her soul to find a smidge of anything that relates to the statements you make.

Sometimes flattery in a reading can even border on flirtation. Patrick Jane has used this technique on several female suspects. In the episode "Ladies in Red," Jane even goes so far as to make a bet with Rigsby that he can seduce a grieving widow. While the woman seems a bit taken aback at first by his forwardness, she quickly begins to confide in him. Jane uses the attraction to gain her trust and later deduces that, in fact, she killed her own husband.

I've certainly used flirtation in my shows, but it's important to keep the exchange professional, or you risk coming off like a creep. In order to use this kind of seduction appropriately, I look for the subject to start the flirtatious exchange. If the subject originates the vibe, then I respond in kind to encourage this rapport to grow. Building this kind of connection with your subject can result in a unique, dynamic performance.

COMMON AREAS OF INTEREST

Another surefire approach to add strength to a reading is to know what areas generally interest most people. While it is true that many people like magic and mentalism, it is much more accurate to say that only a few people actually perform and study mentalism and magic when compared to, say, baseball or sailing.

Recognizing areas of common interest is not as hard as you might first think. There are certain areas and subject matters in life that we as humans simply cannot help but be interested in.

I like to remember these areas by using this acronym: READ ME.

■ R is for Romance and Sex—Little needs to be said here. Everyone, everywhere, no matter what the time or situation, is interested in his or her sex life. Some are more interested in the romance side of things than others, but the interest in sex is pretty universal. Enough said.

■ E is for Education and Wisdom—While this certainly reso- nates stronger with younger people, the general heading holds true for many, many people. Even those who are not currently in a formal educational institution may have to study for work, may have children in school, and so forth.

■ A is for Ambition and Career—Almost everyone in the world has an ambition somewhere in the back of his or her mind. Most often these ambitions are left unrealized. Whether it's to paint that masterpiece or write a novel, humans tend to have ambitions to do something far removed from their day-to-day work, something that they consider being creative and interesting. People also almost always believe they are smarter than most of the people around them. If they are told as much, they will latch on to it. These ambitions are often related to career. Everyone the world over wants his or her job to be safe, fun, and interesting. All people are interested in making their way up the ladder at their place of business.

■ D is for Destination and Travel—Everyone is interested in the notion of visiting new places. This can extend from a simple vacation from work all the way up to throwing your belong- ings into a bag and traveling the world. Almost everyone in the world shares an interest in travel.

- M is for Money and Finance—Love it or hate it, it makes the world go round. People always are interested in money and its role in their lives. This, I feel, might be the most universal of all common areas of interest.

- E is for Energy and Health—I would go as far as to say that everyone in the world is interested in their own wellness and the wellness of those around them. It is an easy assumption to make that health will play a part in your subject's psyche.

Now within these general areas we find other smaller areas of commonality. For example, if one is sitting with a fifty-year-old woman, her concerns about health, money, and education are going to be very different than those of a twenty-four-year-old woman. Chances are, you'll be able to make some general assumptions about similar concerns when the person is standing in front of you.

THE FATHER OF COLD READING

Ray Hyman, a professor of psychology at the University of Oregon and a former mentalist, is known as the modern father of cold reading, having studied the effects it has on an audience. Here are some simple guidelines set forth in his book *The Elusive Quarry: A Scientific Appraisal of Psychical Research*.

The following is a thirteen-point guide to cold reading as outlined by Hyman. Study this guide well and you'll soon be able to amaze your friends with your newfound psychic powers.

1. *Remember to be confident.* Looking like you know what you're doing is almost more important than actually knowing what you're doing. If you believe it, then the person you're reading is more likely to believe it. If you aren't confident and doubt your skills, then your subject in turn will doubt you.

2. *Keep up with the latest statistics.* So much of cold reading is being able to break the ice, and the latest statistics, polls, and surveys can help you achieve that. For instance, if you are able to glean information on a person's religion, vocation, or town of residence, you might be able to use your "psychic" abilities to tell the person how he or she voted in the last election, based on the statistics you've memorized.

3. *Be modest.* Confidence and modesty shouldn't be confused. You can be confident while also being modest. If you set up your subject with a sense of being modest, you'll then be better able to surprise him or her with just how accurate your reading is.

4. *Cooperation is key.* You want to gain cooperation from the subject you're trying to read before you even make your first statement of the reading. Do this by emphasizing that successful reading depends on the subject being able to relay his or her thoughts to you. This also establishes an alibi if the reading doesn't work out. You simply can say the subject wasn't focused enough. But by putting the subject on the spot, you're also forcing the subject to work hard to find some connection in his or her own life with whatever statements you

make. Remember, as I said earlier, they want to make a connection. They want to please you.

5. *Gimmicks are good.* While I make no claim that items like tarot cards and crystal balls aid in a reading, they can give you time as you formulate your questions. They set the atmosphere and draw the attention away from you as the reader. Still, it's important to remember that a gimmick can also become a crutch that gets in the way of developing your own powers of observation.

6. *Have a go-to phrase.* Come up with some go-to phrases or statements that you can always keep in your back pocket when you need something to say or are drawing a blank. Having some stock phrases also helps you in establishing your brand. So think of something creative.

7. *Keep your eyes open.* You need to make sure you're reacting to more than a person's statements. Observing a person's body language, what he or she is wearing, and other mannerisms can prove critical to an effective reading.

8. *Go fishing.* When you go fishing with someone, you're rephrasing something the person has told you and serving it back as a question or a positive assertion. Often the subject will react to that by offering even more information, aiding in your reading. The subject also will tend to forget that he or she was the source of the information in the first place.

9. *Listen before speaking.* No, I'm not talking about your marriage. If you strike a chord with a subject, the subject will likely be busting at the seams to tell you more and more. So make sure you pause your reading long enough to let the person express what he or she wants to express. Often the people being read by a "psychic" will spend more time speaking than the person actually performing the reading.

10. *Be dramatic.* Sometimes you have very little to go on at the beginning of the reading, so you have to make it effective and make it last. So ham it up a little and build up what you've read with big words and verbal scenes.

11. *Pretend you know more.* Have you ever been to the doctor's office and felt like the physician was holding out on some information? That's how you have to act as a reader. Once you are able to convince your subject that you know something about him or her that the subject never would have thought you could know, the subject will believe you know even more.

12. *Flattery will get you everywhere.* As I said earlier, flattering someone and throwing compliments a subject's way will never hurt a reading. There are times when people will try to rebut your positive comments, but you can simply counter with "You're sometimes skeptical of people who try to praise you."

13. *Tell them what they want to hear.* When it comes to cold readings, this is the Golden Rule. People will respond to what they want to hear. So it's your job to figure out just what that is.

MORE FISHING

I wanted to come back to one of the thirteen steps I mentioned above, because I feel it's a critical component to cold readings.

Fishing is basically a form of interrogation that in this case is taking place outside of a police station. With fishing you will both aquire information while also getting your subject to react and, in turn, provide you with more information. After the subject reacts, you'll know, based on the subject's positive or negative reaction, how to proceed.

This concept of fishing is very popular among professionals who claim to be able to speak to the dead. If you've watched any of the television shows where the host makes that claim, I'm sure you've seen this technique used but will only now truly know that it's a mentalist trick.

The fishing technique would go something like this:

You as the reader would say "I'm seeing someone with an R in your life."

If the person gives you any kind of affirmative response, you feed that back to them by saying "Perhaps a Randy or Robbie. I'm seeing R . . ."

Now, remember that I said if you're performing a cold reading correctly, your subject will work hard to make the connection that you're seeking, ignoring the fact that he or she has had to work so hard and ignoring the fact that the connection is distant at best.

So as you prod away at the Rs, you may finally hear your subject proclaim, "Yes! I had a great aunt Ruth!"

Fishing is a skill that's invaluable to a psychic, I mean a mentalist.

When fishing, it's important that you offer positive reinforcement for even the slightest acceptance—either verbal or physical—from your subject about something you've said.

If the person simply offers the slightest head nod when you say, "Someone in your family is having a hard go of it," then you need to quickly follow that up with "Thank you for your confirmation."

This positive reinforcement encourages the subject to be more outgoing, and in turn you will have more material to work from.

■ ■

MENTALIST READING EXERCISE— START WITH THE SUBJECT'S NAME

I like to employ a technique that uses the subject's name and the names of the subject's family members when you begin to read the person. People love nothing more than hearing their name repeated. After you learn how to perform an initial reading, you'll be able to repeat your subject's name and develop an acronym of sorts based on what you read. Of course the acronym would be based, in part, on our Barnum Statements. The reading would sound something like this: " I wonder what 'Simon' means . . ."

■ "S. I think S stands for the smiling disposition that you have deep down."

■ "The I in your name stands for several things. It stands for the incredible feelings of care you have on the inside, but on your outside you tend to not let them come out—you create more of a barrier against these internal feelings coming out."

■ "M stands for money and the gifts of magnetism you have that will cause you to reach and achieve the monetary desires you pursue."

■ "O indicates to me the never-ending circle of O. Your diligence and pursuit of excellence is unparalleled, and your abilities find you very good at figuring out how to continually retry situations in which you have not had the best of luck. The saying that only an insane person will try the same thing over and over and expect different results comes to mind. You are not that person. You will repeatedly try to astonish and amaze."

■ "N stands for the fact that no one is right for you. Unfortunately you have a challenge in love, and since you have such a perfectionist attitude, you will be scouring the planet looking for the right one for you."

■ ■

PEOPLE ARE A PARADOX

When you're reading someone, you really need to think about your own personality and how someone could read you.

Is there really any one personality trait that really describes you, or are you a combination of traits? And are some of those traits directly in conflict with one another? Are you outgoing in large crowds and very reserved with your family? Are you confident in business settings but secretly doubtful of your own skills and talents?

Take those factors into account when reading someone. You basically want to make opposite statements directly after one another. While, as I stated above, many people actually do believe that their lives reflect these opposite statements, an additional benefit of saying both things is that you have to hit on one of them. And as I said, people generally will have such a desire to find a purpose in your reading that they'll ignore the portion that you didn't hit on.

So here's what your reading may sound like when making these opposite statements:

"You are really a combination of things. Part of you likes to be outgoing, and you can be really energetic and the life of the party. But there is another part of you that likes to stay at home and relax and just be with somebody you like and have quiet times. And you can be a homebody at the same time. I see both those sides in you. Perhaps one of them is more dominant."

If that reading was made about you, would it be accurate? And would your response be to quickly tell the reader which trait was more dominant, giving him or her more material to work with?

I think so!

COLD READING SCRIPT

I now will present you with a classic script for a cold reading. This basically is the final summary of how you might describe the person you're reading. Note the number of Barnum Statements in this script. Also note how these statements seem to ring so true in your own life.

Imagine someone was describing you when making these statements. You might think the reading bordered on spooky and supernatural. However, we know it is nothing more than a clever mentalist at work.

"Some of your aspirations tend to be pretty unrealistic. At times you are extroverted, affable, sociable, while at other times you are introverted, wary, and reserved. You have found it unwise to be too frank in revealing yourself to others. You pride yourself on being an independent thinker and do not accept others' opinions without satisfactory proof. You prefer a certain amount of change and variety, and become dissatisfied when hemmed in by restrictions and limitations. At times you have serious doubts as to whether you have made the right decision or done the right thing. Disciplined and controlled on the outside, you tend to be worrisome and insecure on the inside.

"Your sexual adjustment has presented some problems for you. While you have some personality weaknesses, you are generally able to compensate for them. You have a great deal of unused capacity which you have not turned to your advantage. You have a tendency to be critical of yourself. You have a strong need for other people to like you and for them to admire you.

"People close to you have been taking advantage of you. Your basic honesty has been getting in your way. Many opportunities that you have had offered to you in the past have had to be surrendered because you refuse to take advantage of others. You like to read books and articles to improve your mind. In fact, if you're not already in some sort of personal service business, you should be. You have an infinite capacity for understanding people's problems and you can sympathize with them. But you are firm when confronted with obstinacy or outright stupidity. Law enforcement would be another field you understand. Your sense of justice is quite strong."

You'll be surprised how many people will think you've had a peek inside their heads after you've shared this reading with them. You'll be able to convince people you've just met that you know as much about them as they know about themselves.

Now you know the secrets of the world's best "psychics." Cold reading isn't about magical powers or mental telepathy, it's about educating yourself on specific generalizations and statistics and letting the subject's feedback guide you.

You can use these tips to become the next Patrick Jane, or at least to score a few free drinks when you entertain some friends at a local bar.

Hot Readings

I mentioned at the very beginning of this chapter that there are two main types of readings: cold readings and hot readings.

Hot readings are performed by professionals who are able to gather information about you before you sit down for your reading. How do they do this?

Well the easiest way is for them to schedule an appointment with you. If you've prescheduled someone for a reading, then you have a lot of time to learn about them. You can gather information in a number of ways.

Perhaps someone will give you a fact about the person in conversation. For example, "Simon is a Scorpio and drives a red Porsche." During the reading you'll be able to elaborate on the subject's personality based on what you know about Scorpio traits and generalizations about individuals who drive expensive, showy cars.

You can watch the person for a period of time and pick up things from their movements and appearance. With a hot reading, you'll have more time to make observations than in an on-the-spot cold reading. Maybe you'll note that the person goes outside for smoking breaks or wears a watch on his or her right wrist, meaning the person is probably left-handed.

Finally, you may overhear bits of the subject's conversations with others. Perhaps you'll hear the person say, "Yes, we love that place. We go to Hawaii every spring because my sister-in-law has a house there." Again, you can use this information to make your deductions about that individual.

Personally, my schedule doesn't allow for hot readings. I'm usually afforded very little time between traveling to my scheduled event and walking into the show. There's really no opportunity for me to obtain the "hot" information, and if I tried, the research would have to be rushed and then it wouldn't be very dependable.

I find cold reading more effective anyway. By trusting your own instincts and powers of observation, you can use the information that's right in front of you. It's more immediate and often more accurate.

Leading Readings

Earlier in this chapter I mentioned that I combine cold readings with something that I call a leading reading.

So what is a leading reading?

Well if cold and hot readings are considered tools that allow you to tell someone about his or her present life, and maybe dive a bit into the past, a leading reading would be a look into that person's future.

Essentially, a leading reading suggests likely future scenarios for your subject. This way, the reader is "predicting" future events and experiences which, by the mere fact that you've introduced them into someone's psyche, are more likely to come true for that person.

The subject now is looking for these future scenarios everywhere he or she goes.

YOU WILL COME ACROSS AN OPPORTUNITY

So what does a leading reading sound like?

Chances are if you've been to a psychic or overheard a psychic reading, you've been privy to a reading that's been led in a future direction. For instance, it might sound something like this:

"You are going to soon meet a woman in a black business suit and carrying a black bag. She will offer you a business opportunity. Don't take it. She will contact you again and offer you a much better deal, and it's OK to take that one."

While the leading reading I just described may have been a little specific, it wasn't so impressively specific if you know the person you're dealing with.

Perhaps this leading reading stemmed from the cold reading of a business executive from a large company. It's likely that there's a powerful woman in that company that our subject deals with, and she likely has a black suit and bag. From there it's a matter of the subject looking for the "opportunity."

There's a saying that goes: "If you're a hammer, then all you'll find in people is nails."

Well the same goes for these leading readings. If the subject is looking for an opportunity, then it's likely the subject will find opportunities everywhere he or she looks. Would the subject have found these opportunities if he or she hadn't been read? Or would they have simply come and gone, with the subject giving little notice? Well I guess that's a secret for us mentalists.

So how do you perform leading readings?

Well the trick is to get the most information possible out of your cold reading and then use those observations and accurate hits to move the person forward.

Is someone struggling with depression? Then tell that person that a good listener will come into his or her life, and that communicating his or her problems to this person will make the subject feel better. The subject now will be looking for this person, and will feel better after speaking with him or her.

Be as specific as you feel comfortable being based on what you've learned about the person.

Now that we've added readings to our toolbox, how do we bring all of our skills together to become true mentalists?

Guessing Games

Despite all that I've taught you, there's one skill, a final piece of the puzzle, that seems too simple but should never be left out of your mentalist toolbox: Don't be afraid to guess!

Your guess, of course, will be based on statistical truths—for instance most people have a scar on their right knee—but it will be a guess nonetheless.

Often Patrick Jane will make use of statements that will apply to many, many people (see Appendix A) and mix these in with the other observations he has made. Part of this is just plain good psychology, but it's also partially a guess.

Patrick makes "educated guesses" in every episode of *The Mentalist*. The act of "cold reading" is essentially all about guessing.

The key is to "own" the statements you're making, whether or not you are sure you're right. The expression "fake it till you make it" applies here. While the skill of people-reading lies in our ability to be observant and to "watch closely," if you begin to incorporate certain statistical truths in educated guesses, it will almost guarantee an accurate hit or two, and you'll have a leg up on your subject.

You may need to weed through some of your guesses before you share them with your subject. If you go with the most probable statement first, it can lead to feedback from the person that will tell you if your next guess is right.

Patrick Jane's brain is always working, always running through possible theories and scenarios, but he picks and chooses which ones to share with his partners. When Lisbon asks him why he didn't share his hunch with her on a case, he responds, "If I told you about every hunch, you'd get very irritated."

I know of no better quicker way to begin a successful reading than to get lucky and hit on a correct response. You see, if we are instantly very insightful and successful with our observations of a person, then this person is more likely to accept other observations or to express him- or herself clearly. With that communication the person will allow us to deduce various other pieces of information. The illusion of success, initiated through a guess, often can lead to real success.

Don't think guessing works?

Go to the Web site http://www.mysticalball.com/ and ask the virtual mystical ball a question. Or do the same with a Magic 8 Ball. People who read mystical balls are doing nothing more than performing cold readings, just with a ball in front of them. It's the same concept.

When I went to this virtual mystical ball Web site, it requested that I ask a yes-or-no question. So I asked, "Am I a man?"

The mystical ball answered "yes."

A couple of more questions down the line the ball fell flat on its face with its answers. The Web site obviously generates yes, no, and maybe responses based on a random calculation. But for me, a mentalist, it guessed right on the first question.

How about that for the power of guessing?

CHAPTER EIGHT

Tricks of the Trade

At this point in the book, I've armed you with all of the most valuable mentalist tools. You know how to prime your brain to think as smart and efficiently as possible. You know how to tune in to your surroundings and observe with all of your senses. You've learned the best techniques for growing your memory and acquiring amazing powers of recall. You're ready to practice your lie detection skills so that you can always see through to the truth. You know exactly how to look, act, and feel in order to take control of an audience or situation. You're able to entrance someone and plant post-hypnotic suggestions. And you can read a complete stranger in such a way that that stranger may think you've been living inside his or her head.

Now that you have all of these tools, you're prepared to

learn some of the tricks of the trade. If you practice and hone all of these mentalist skills, you'll be able to amaze and entertain friends with your incredible feats. It's time to put the rookie mentalist to work.

Sight Without Sight

In Episode 16 of Season 1 of *The Mentalist* ("Bloodshot"), Jane is blinded by an accident and has to wear bandages over his eyes for the entire episode, but that doesn't stop him from having an uncanny ability to read people and understand the situation around him.

In fact, Jane, in a blind state, probably has stronger observations skills than we have with full use of our sight and all our other senses.

Going back to the "Bloodshot" episode; Jane temporarily loses his sight but finds he hasn't lost his ability to observe and understand everything that is going on around him. Mentalists around the world often use their powers of observation to wow a crowd by covering their eyes and reading the person and situation in front of them.

It's a pretty common mentalist trick.

I recall when Johnny Carson had a famous psychic on *The Tonight Show*, and the psychic was going to bandage up his head and have Johnny hide something, then the illusionist would reveal the object's location. And Johnny simply said something like "No, that's OK, we don't have to go through all that. I trust you aren't looking. Just turn your head."

Needless to say the experiment failed, as this totally threw the psychic's presentation off. He wasn't prepared for that one—or the fact that Johnny Carson was actually a trained magician. Johnny knew that in this case the psychic would be able to see through the blindfold. He also knew that the psychic/mentalist would use his calm and power over the crowd to make people think that he couldn't see through the blindfold, to make people think they were witnessing some miraculous event.

But that doesn't mean that every time a mentalist or magician does this trick, you should be skeptical of its legitimacy. Not every mentalist uses a translucent blindfold. Honestly, most of them do not.

This is a good trick to get some help with. Ask one of your friends to act as your assistant. Make sure you choose someone tight-lipped and trustworthy. The trick and the element of mystery will be spoiled if your friend reveals all of your secrets after the show is over.

You'll need to practice a bit with your assistant in advance. It's not a job that can be handed over at the last minute. The two of you will need to confer and develop a strategy. Basically you need to establish a code.

Let's say you blindfold yourself and your assistant holds a pen in front of you. The assistant then asks, "I am holding an object in front of you. Please explore it now."

After a couple of seconds, and of course, a certain amount of dramatic flair, you announce that it's a pen. But how could you have done that while blindfolded? Well you and your assistant had worked out that the first letter of each word in the last sentence the assistant spoke would be used to identify the object. Since there's no such thing as a "pein," you were quickly able to surmise that the object was a pen.

This is a pretty easy trick that can be adapted to the performer. After a little practice you and an assistant can have this down cold. Just as long as someone doesn't give your assistant an E-L-E-P-H-A-N-T to hold up or, worse, a map of M-I-S-S-I-S-S-I-P-P-I. But make no mistake, the more complex your code is, the harder it will be for an audience to recognize its use. So to really wow an audience you want to find a good assistant and practice this blindfold trick for a long while with an extremely complex code.

HIDDEN OBJECT

Here's another great trick for discovering a hidden object or who may be concealing it.

Let's say you take off your watch and give it to a member of the audience. You tell that person that you're going to go into a back room, and while you're gone you want the person to give the watch to another member of the audience. When you return, you'll be able to identify who is holding the watch.

Another seemingly impossible task, isn't it?

Well not really.

We've already discussed how we can uncover a lot of information about people simply through their facial expressions, and we know that someone's body language can tell us whether that person is lying or telling the truth.

And then, of course, from our cold reading instruction, we know all about how someone's outward actions can tell us how that person feels on the inside.

These are all tools that you can use to perform this hidden object trick.

So now you've given the object to someone and walked away from the audience, having instructed the person to give the object to someone else.

What will you do when you return? Well I guarantee that the person now holding the object will be offering some tells. Most likely, the person will be trying so hard to look like he or she is not holding the object that the person will look completely awkward and unnatural.

This audience member likely will be avoiding eye contact with you and trying to look nonchalant. Most people can't look nonchalant without actually being nonchalant. When they try to act in a way that's not natural, they just look odd, and you'll likely be able to pick that up.

The trick is not to stare at someone, but to use your peripheral vision to see how someone is acting when you're not looking directly at them. If you stare directly into someone's eyes, then that person is going to stare right back at you, he or she really has no choice. But if you're a couple of people away from the person who is holding the object and you observe them from the corner of your eye, you'll probably notice that that person is working to avoid your glance, or even moving his or her entire body away from you.

But it's not only the person holding the object who will offer the tells that can help you uncover the truth. You also can read the body language of the people around that person.

Again, using your peripheral vision, look to see if they are sneaking glances over to a particular person? Are they moving their bodies away from a particular person? More importantly, do they appear very normal when you look at them, and not giving off that sense of fake, awkward nonchalance? The normalcy alone will eliminate them as someone who's concealing something, while all the other tells will be icing on the cake.

The hidden object trick can be fun and isn't too difficult to master if you take the time to practice. You'll get better and better at this trick as you spend more time observing people and their tells.

THE SEALED ENVELOPE

So how about a second Johnny Carson reference in this chapter?

Probably one of Johnny's most popular acts was when he performed as Carnac the Magnificent. As Carnac, Johnny would hold a sealed envelope to his head and offer an answer to an unknown question. Then he would open the envelope to reveal the question—which was, no doubt, hilarious—and laughter from the audience would follow.

Here's an example:

Johnny holds the envelope to his head and says: "Over 105 in Los Angeles."

He then opens the envelope and reads: "Under the Reagan plan, how old would you have to be to collect Social Security?"

OK, so it was probably funnier in the eighties.

While Johnny obviously knows what is in the envelopes, which are part of his act, this sort of trick isn't foreign to mentalists and is derived from what's called billet reading. These billet readings involve the magician, like Johnny, already knowing or in some way being tipped off to what's in the envelope.

In most cases an assistant is planted in the audience to help with the exercise. A number of audience members are each asked to write something on a slip of paper, place it in an envelope, and seal it. The "plant" will be one of the people selected to write something down. When collecting the envelopes, the mentalist will be sure to place the plant's envelope at the bottom of the pile.

The plant and the mentalist will have already agreed on what would be written in that envelope. For the sake of this example, let's say they wrote, "I'm afraid of clowns." So the mentalist will pick up the first envelope and perhaps put it up to his forehead, pretending to see what's written inside with his mind.

"Hmmmmm . . . I'm sensing some fear . . . It seems to be

related to a child's toy or something . . . A clown! That's it. This person has a fear of clowns!"

Then he'll open the first envelope—which is actually the note from another audience member—and pretend to read aloud that it states "I'm afraid of clowns." In the meantime, he's reading the next person's answer and committing it to memory. When he picks up the second envelope, he'll use the information that he just read to pretend that he's reading the next one. The audience member will confirm with amazement that he's correct. It's very important that the mentalist never let the audience see what's really written on each of the pieces of paper or the jig is up!

This is a rather elaborate trick and requires quite a bit of setup and a decent-sized audience to perform effectively. But by using some of the same techniques that you've learned in the cold reading chapter, you can perform some of your own impressive sealed envelope tricks. Basically what you're trying to do is become a human Magic 8 Ball. You want the person asking the question that will go in the envelope to ask something that can be answered with a yes or a no, and then you want to offer vague answers that resonate with the subject enough to make that person feel like the two of you have connected.

I talk about Magic 8 Balls a little later in the book, but isn't it amazing how often they're indeed right? Sure, they're vague, but they're right. You're smarter than an 8 Ball, aren't you?

So through what you pick up and read about the subject, and the brief conversation you have with that person before he or she writes a yes-or-no question on a piece of paper and places it in the envelope, you should be able to get a good idea of what this person is going to ask, or what answer he or she is looking for.

Does the person seem to be generally positive and energetic? If so, then the question they ask likely will be one that will require a positive response—a Yes!

Are they negative and skeptical? Then you'll probably want to answer with a no. But those are just the basics. If you use the Barnum Statements you've already learned, then you'll have all the ammunition you need.

THE NOSE KNOWS

In this demonstration you seemingly become a human lie detector, just like Patrick Jane.

Have a friend hold a folded up dollar bill behind his or her back, placed in either the right hand or the left hand. With it hidden in one hand, have the person move both hands in front, with their fists tightly clenched so that no one can see which hand the dollar bill is in.

Then tell your friend to answer yes to each question you ask, explaining that one of the yes answers will indeed be a lie, but that you will be able to tell the lie from the truth.

And so you ask:

"Is the bill in your right hand?" followed by "Is the bill in your left hand?"

As you requested, the person should offer a yes response to

each question. Despite you having no way of knowing which of the hands the bill rests in, you will be able to find it each time.

So how will you know which hand? This secret is so simple that at first glance you might pass up the true power that exists within it.

Mentalism is all about paying close attention to what someone's body displays without that person even being aware of it. This happens all of the time. We do it all of the time.

Have you ever felt like you knew something but did not know how you knew it? There is a likelihood this was due to your reading nonverbal communication without even being aware you were doing so.

You see, we all read the thoughts of others, and this happens every day. If we did not, we would not be able to function in the complex world we live in. A shrug carries a whole different set of signals than a smile. While that's an obvious example, when we begin to look deeper, we find that a whole host of nonverbal communications exist beneath the surface.

No one has better developed these skills than Paul Ekman, who studied facial expressions across cultures. His findings proved that regardless of our age, race, gender, or even cultural background, there are a set of universal actions we all display without even knowing we are doing so. You can find out more about his work in his book *Emotions Revealed*.

One of these "universal tells" is at the heart of this trick. This simple demonstration is rooted in evolutionary psychology and in one simple fact: The nose knows.

I know that doesn't make sense to you right now, so just give me a moment to prove my point.

Take an object, place it behind your back, and hide it in one of your hands, just as we had someone else do with the dollar bill. Now, with that object hidden in one of your fists, bring your hands back in front of you.

Take a deep breath in and pay attention to the direction your nose is pointing. Your nose knows which hand the object is hidden in, and it's pointing in that direction. Simple, isn't it?

Have a friend do this a few times and pay close attention to the direction in which your friend's nose points. You will find that while this is a subtle and small piece of nonverbal communication, with a little work you will be able to use it to instantly reveal within which hand an object is hidden.

I imagine you can get someone to pay for several rounds at the bar if you base the beer tab on you being able to perform this little trick.

While the nose knows, you also want to pay close attention to the clenched fists. You often will find that your guess based on the direction the person's nose is pointing is also confirmed by that hand becoming slightly flushed with blood. This is due to the fact that the object hidden within is being tightly gripped, while the other hand remains empty. This causes a stronger flow of blood to the hand concealing the object.

So now that you've got this down, it's time to add smoke to the mirrors.

You see, a true mentalist will leave the audience guessing. So instead of simply saying, "Your nose points in this direction," add some theatrical flair to the event by claiming to be able to read a host of other nonverbal signals and touting yourself as a human lie detector.

Read the descriptions of this demonstration a few times and think about how you will add some smoke and mirrors. Maybe you claim to be able to read the subject's eye movements, or maybe it's something that's triggered by the way you ask the question. Whatever you decide, make sure you add your own style and some theatrical flair to this simple demonstration of mentalism.

FREE WILL?

For this next trick, you'll begin by placing a written prediction on the table. You then ask your subject to conduct a "personality" test with you. You ask the subject to answer three questions without thinking. Sure enough when the prediction is checked, you will have seemingly foretold the exact way the subject would think long before he or she was doing it!

Again, with this exercise we find ourselves presented with a simple but devious exploitation of human nature. In this demonstration we make use of naturally occurring statistical favor. Every choice we make in some way is affected by our psychology. Often it is possible to cause someone to make the choice that you want him or her to make by simply wording the question in a certain way.

In the mentalist trade, this method is known as psychological force. We will use three of this type of question in this demonstration.

Predict the Future

Start this demonstration by stating a prediction. You might want to add something witty or interesting to the beginning of the prediction to personalize it for your subject, however that is not necessary.

In this example the meat of the prediction that you write down must include the following:

> "If my skills are well honed this evening, you will have no other option than to think of the color blue, the number seven, and a rose."

Write this prediction on a sheet of paper that is thick enough not to allow the ink to bleed through and then seal it in some kind of container or place it in your wallet.

Now when the time comes to perform this demonstration, remove your wallet and explain that you would like to play a personality game with your spectator. At this point do not mention the prediction or any intent of predicting the outcome of the choices you will present your audience member with. You need the subject to be natural and relaxed in his or her decisions, in order for you to take advantage of the psychological forces.

To mention a prediction or any intention of controlling the way the subject thinks would cause the subject to change his or her way of thinking and likely ruin the outcome of the demonstration.

Begin by explaining:

"We are going to play a game. In a moment I will snap my fingers each time I ask you a question. These are simple questions, so please answer them without thinking. Literally the first thought that pops into your mind."

Now continue after a brief pause:

"A color"

Immediately snap your fingers when you ask this question, it will encourage your spectator to hurry with the answer and not to overthink the decision-making process. Ninety-nine times out of a hundred, when someone is asked in this fashion to name a color, that person will respond blue.

Continue this with the next question:

"A number between one and ten."

Once again snap your fingers to encourage a hurried response. Seven is the most common answer and will be correct at least 95 percent of the time.

Or for a more advanced version of this, try:

"Name a number between one and one hundred in which both digits are odd and they are not the same digit. So a number like fifteen is OK, but a number like eleven is not. I am focusing on the number right now!"

Can you guess the number? It will almost always be thirty-five or thirty-seven!

Finally ask for:

"A long-stemmed flower."

Once again snap your fingers to encourage a hurried response. A rose is the most common answer, and it will be correct at least 99 percent of the time.

Now reveal your prediction and explain:

"I was actually trying to control the way you think. However in the process I think I have learned a little about how you think. I recorded my target thoughts, the ones I was trying to influence your mind into deciding upon right here in my wallet."

Remove your prediction and accept your glory as a mind control expert.

Now, I am indeed a mentalist, so I know right now you are reading this and thinking, "What if they do not name the forced thoughts that I wrote down?"

Well this is why we begin by explaining the two of you will conduct a personality test. You see if they do not name the forced thoughts, you still conclude by saying:

"Well that's interesting, we all think in different ways, and now I think I know a little about how your mind works from the answers you gave to our personality test. In fact I think I know enough to try something very special with you."

You can forgo revealing your predictions and move on to the next trick. Dodging the bullet, you've retained the air of mystery with the personality test and now are ready to move into either the "nose knows" trick previously taught or the next item, which is 100 percent surefire and allows you to look like you know exactly what someone is thinking by neatly hiding a simple magic trick under the guise of mind reading.

POKER FACE

To prepare for this next trick, you must first place four sevens and the king of diamonds on the top of your deck of cards, and then place all the cards back in the box.

When your friends arrive, tell them that you just saw a television show about "reading tells" at the poker table and you want to see if it works. Take out the deck and just deal the top five cards facedown in front of one of them. Tell your friend to take any card at random, and then put the other four back in the deck without looking at them. There is now one facedown card in front of your friend, and you know it is either a king of diamonds or a seven. Ask your friend to peek at the card, the same way one would look at a hole card in a real game.

Say "It's a high card." If he smiles or instantly replies "yes," you know it must be the king. You've learned all you need to know. After some dramatics, declare that your friend has drawn the king of diamonds. Everyone will be amazed.

The seven is a central value in the deck, so if your friend has a seven, he or she is most likely going to hesitate, rather than blurt out "no." If your friend hesitates, you can add "higher than a five." Your friend must agree.

Now you are going to try and determine the suit with only two more statements.

1. You say, "It is a red card." If your friend's response is "yes," then follow with "It is a diamond." If your friend says, "yes," you can now say "It is the seven of diamonds." If your friend says, "no," you conclude with "It is the seven of hearts."

2. If your friend's response to "It is a red card" is "no," you do the same thing with the black suits. "It is a club." If "yes," you name the seven of clubs, if "no," you name the seven of spades.

With a little practice, this can look like you are really reading your subject and finding out the chosen card with uncanny ease and accuracy. The key is to use your own "poker face." Don't make the trick look too easy or you'll be found out.

Now that I've shared how you can use everything I've taught you to entertain your friends, let's talk a little more about how you can use these techniques to manage your day-to-day life.

CHAPTER NINE

The Everyday Mentalist

So far in this book you have been presented with separate skills ranging from strengthening your memory to hypnosis, lie detection, and cold readings.

But the real secret to making use of these skills in your own life, and to becoming a real-life version of Patrick Jane, is to be able to collect all of them under one umbrella and use them at the right moment in your everyday life.

Mentalism is power.

Mentalism is a battle, and in life's battle for power, victory will go to those who find the right weapons and use them.

I have given you the weapons, and now it's just a matter of you training with them, and choosing the right ones to use while in battle.

Power isn't just about being able to call someone and tell that person what to do; it's also about other people seeking you out for your business or wanting to associate with you.

Are you someone who seems to possess a wide knowledge of the world and an awareness of trends?

Are you the early bird who catches sight of opportunities first? Are you someone who's capable of handling many different kinds of situations?

If you are, people will seek you out. They will want to be part of your life and in turn will be more susceptible to the power that you're trying to exert over them.

They'll invite you to vacation at their country homes, to meet their influential associates, to join their social clubs and their business syndicates. And when they do, all of these will enhance your image of power, and widen your power base so you can zoom in even more. The more you build your image as a powerful person, the more powerful you actually become.

So how can you exercise this power in you day-to-day life? Here's how you can bring a bit of your inner mentalist into everything you do.

Always Be Prepared

All of the skills that I've detailed for you can and should be practiced. Whether its cold reading or memory skills or lie detection, you can't simply run into a situation blind and ill prepared. You need to spend hours upon hours refining your skills in order to wield them with confidence. Remember, confidence goes a long way toward becoming an effective mentalist. If you're confident in yourself, others will be confident in you and will try to find their role in your life and connect with what you're telling them.

How else do you use these tools to your full potential?

Well you need to prepare for any situation that you're walking into. This isn't quite the same as a hot reading, but it's preparation nonetheless. There's a good chance you'll know the type of person you'll be dealing with when walking into a room. A bar has a much different atmosphere and clientele than someone's fortieth birthday party at a corporate office. In knowing the people and the atmosphere and the end goal, you'll know how to prepare yourself.

Always keep your eyes and all senses open. If there's one word that I could use to sum up the entire field of mentalism and everything I've tried to get across in this book, it has to be "observation." The better you become at observing the world around you, the better mentalist you'll be.

Remember, observation isn't simply about what's directly in front of you, it's also about what's in your peripheral view. It can be very powerful to be able to watch someone when the person doesn't know he or she is being watched. And just as important is what you hear, smell, taste, and feel when people don't think you're paying attention.

But just because you know everything about someone else doesn't mean you should let them know everything about you.

Keep Them Guessing

You're probably familiar with the phrase "Keep your cards close to the vest."

Why do people say that? Why is it effective?

If you keep your cards close to you, not allowing others to see them, you're keeping your subject wondering what you're up to, what you have up your sleeve.

Once you've said everything you need to say, or shown all your cards, there's no longer a sense of wonderment. People no longer are wanting to know what's on your mind, and what you have to offer.

But by simply being silent and keeping certain aspects about yourself hidden, you can act from a position of power because you're keeping your subject on his or her toes.

So how do you achieve this without coming off as rude or aloof or just plain weird?

Well it can be as simple as making a conscious decision not to share certain things about yourself with other people. Tell yourself, "I'm not going to offer details about my job or my childhood." You can still be friendly and talkative, but you'll restrict the things you talk about. At first, new acquaintances might not even notice. Most people just want to talk about themselves anyway. Really want to be mysterious? If you routinely share a cab home with someone, always ask that you be dropped off on the corner. And then when you get out, start walking in the opposite direction from where the person thinks your home is. As time goes on, the other person will start to wonder about you, and whatever areas of your life you decide to keep hidden will create a sense of secrecy that will throw people off.

Be One Step Ahead

Now that you've got everybody's attention, you can really start to make some power plays. The following strategies will tip the scales in your favor in many social or business situations. This is where you start to exert some of that authority.

FAVORS

You ever see one of those old mafia movies where someone says you never want a mafia type to do a favor for you because then you'll always be in the guy's debt, and he'll hold that over you?

Or what about *The Godfather*, when Don Corleone's second in command says, "Mr. Corleone never asks a second favor once he's refused the first, understood?"

Now, I'm not telling you only to perform favors in order to gain control over someone, but in the context of this chapter it is a useful tool. Favors can be very powerful things, and if you perform one for someone, then that person will always be wondering when you'll ask to be paid back.

I'm not talking about lending someone $1. That's not a favor of large enough magnitude. And it's important that you understand that the magnitude of the favor can only be measured by the person it's being granted to. While you may think something is pretty trivial, the person to whom you're granting the favor could think it's a monumental task.

So basically when asked to do a favor, consider what you can receive in return if you grant the favor. Perhaps if you stay late to help someone to complete a project, that person will give you a recommendation for another position. In fact, why not offer to perform a favor before even being asked. That may really boggle someone's mind and leave him or her thinking, "I wonder what this person wants from me." Maybe you'll never even call in that chit. But that person's appreciation can be a powerful thing in and of itself.

SUBLIMINAL MIND CONTROL

Look up mind control online or in the library and you'll find a lot of references to subliminal mind control. For instance one article might suggest that a strong vocabulary will make someone think more of you and leave you in a better position to control that person. Or you might find a suggestion that you play to someone's emotions by telling the person a sad or romantic story.

While these tactics might work, I really wouldn't consider them subliminal, because they're not tactics that are circumventing the conscious mind. It's not as if the person in front of you doesn't know you're using the big words, or doesn't understand that the story you're telling them is an emotional one. They get that, and it's likely resonating with them on a very conscious level. It's not as if every person who tells another person an emotional story is trying to exert some sort of mind control.

But when you use these tools in the right situation, you can indeed use them to take control.

Pick Your Battles

When you're dealing with someone who is open-minded and your powers of persuasion have been working from the moment you first started talking, all of your mentalist tools will do their work and everything will line up in your favor.

But what if you're dealing with someone whose mind is closed to your ideas and influence from the start, or who feels he or she is in direct competition with you? Then things must be handled somewhat differently.

Most important, be in control of the situation at all times. If you feel your control is slipping, do something to regain it. You could do something vividly dramatic and totally bewildering to the other person, like suddenly shouting or pounding on your desk. Or you could press a secret buzzer to have someone rush in and interrupt when the other side is coming on too strong.

Never ever get into a power struggle when you're at any kind of a disadvantage. If you're tired, or if the discussion turns to a subject in which the other person is an expert, then you need to bale.

Always focus your own mental energy and project your

thoughts into the other person's mind. Look him or her in the eyes and try to gain the person's confidence. Always envision a victory that is even bigger than your immediate goal.

And whatever you do, don't lose; that is, if you realize that you can't beat the other person, leave. It's better not to have victory than to have a defeat.

Putting It into Practice

These mentalist techniques can come in handy in many different everyday situations, but I'll show you just how. One profession that could really benefit from these skills is sales. Let's explore the mentalist as salesperson.

Gaining power over someone often requires telling the person what he or she wants to hear. But the trick is to figure out just what that is. So you'll start out by giving the other person basic information about what you're selling. What does it do? What service does it offer? What are the benefits of the product or person?

You then continue with your sales approach, always watching the other person's reactions carefully. When you see the person's eyes light up and he or she leans forward with interest, then continue on the topic that aroused that interest, no matter how odd it may seem to you. And do the opposite if at any time your customer shows less than the normal amount of interest, that is, shorten that part of your pitch and go on to the next.

Peer pressure and a sense of demand often helps in selling something. "Well, Mr. Brown from the office down the street said he'll buy ten and sees it having a lot of value." But you always have to balance that with the danger of your bluff being called. Don't let yourself get caught in a fib.

Now suppose the person you're dealing with seems convinced but can't make up his or her mind to actually hand over the money or sign the contract. In this instance, you can exert your power by implying that the person obviously can't afford this item, or doesn't have the authority to make a decision. This needs to be done with a certain amount of finesse. Instead of just angering the customer, you want to put the customer on the defensive, to force the customer to prove to you that he or she is indeed a person of authority. It's sort of like those rams who bump horns in the wild to assert their dominance. Don't underestimate the power of someone's pride.

Basically, you need to do whatever it takes to close the deal. If, however, you realize you're attempting the impossible, then you need to be in control of when the negotiations end.

Say you're in an interview for a job and you sense that it's not going well. You know you're not going to get this job, and the next fifteen minutes of this interview will solely be for the purpose of this exec being able to fill out all the paperwork that documents that he or she gave you a fair opportunity.

Well what if instead of continuing with that failed interview you stand up and say, "We both know I'm not getting this job. I appreciate your time and wish you well."

What would that accomplish?

Well you were pretty sure you weren't going to get the job before you said anything, so there really wasn't anything lost there. But maybe, just maybe, this exec now wonders about you and thinks, "If this person could act with that much confidence, maybe that's someone I want working for me."

Or maybe the executive thinks highly enough of you to suggest you for another job.

Either way, you've left this person wondering about you, and you've left with yourself in control of the situation.

You're Ready

So I've shared my secrets.

Have I shared all of them? What kind of question is that to ask a mentalist? Of course not. If I did, I wouldn't be much of a mentalist.

But I've certainly shared enough to allow you to achieve your mentalist goals. The power is within your grasp. It's up to you to grab it.

So keep your weapons handy; get a head start and don't lose it. Be alert for clues you can use to your advantage, and carry yourself with confidence.

Broadcast your power, and speak and move with assurance.

And most important, by whatever means necessary, get your message across. If you're able to manage that without your subject realizing it, then you've become a true mentalist.

Generalizations That Apply to Many People

- Most people feel that they have had a premonition at some point in their lives.

- A lot of people claim that before a death or disaster they "felt in their bones" that it was coming.

- When women go shopping they tend to be as curious about other shoppers as they are about the products.

- Most people see themselves as nice and of sincere judgment.

- Most people have a distaste for insincerity.

- Most men feel they are resourceful and would make a good candidate for *Survivor*.

- Most women have wondered about the possibility of "what if I had twins" and have had a miscarriage or have feared that they might have had one.

- Most women have contemplated writing a children's book.

- The most common birthday is October 5.

- The least common birthday is May 22.

- Most people forget that not everyone has the abilities that they have grown up with.

- Most people have a scar on their right knee. *You can further add to the odds of this hitting by noting which hand is dominant. Remember these techniques all build upon one another, and we can deduce which hand is more prominent from the way someone ties a tie, fastens a belt, or adjusts a pair of glasses. If the dominant hand is right, the chances are the scar will be on the left knee. If the dominant hand is left, the chances are the scar will be on the right knee.*

- Tall, thin people have been known to complain more often about having back pain or problems.

- Most older single men have a fear of "being a meal ticket" in a relationship and consequently build up an air of confidence and independence, but secretly will harbor feelings of loneliness.

- People avoid things that they do not understand.

- People often do not want to understand what they do not like.

- People often will pretend to understand something in order to move a situation forward and not admit to being confused.

- It is common for most people to agree to the statement "You had trouble dealing with your father when you were growing up."

- Eighty-one percent of adults have some problem with their feet.

- Women who wear high heels at work suffer from several kinds of foot maladies.

- Most women wonder if they are better kissers than their husbands or boyfriends.

- Many redheads suffer from seasonal allergies.

- Most people have been found to have one leg shorter than the other.

- California residents see themselves as healthier than those living in their neighboring states.

- Most car accidents happen within one mile of a person's home or residence.

- Most people feel they are more ethical than others.

- Most day traders or stock market professionals think that their stock picking abilities are far better than those of their associates.

- Most women feel that their feet are too large.

- Most men fear rejection.

- Most men love Sundays.

- And obviously most people dislike Mondays.

- Most people fear giving a presentation to a live audience.

- Most people hate the sound of their own voice when it has been audio recorded.

- Most older men have had heart palpitations.

- Most people have had their heart broken a few times.

- Most short people have a Napoleon complex or inferiority complex.

- Most celebrities deeply fear they will lose it all.

- Most wealthy people fear they will lose it all—usually the richer they are, the deeper the fear.

- Most people know someone or are close with someone whose name begins with the letter J.

- Most people think and feel that they are overweight.

- Most men are supersensitive/protective of some female figure—either Mom, a girlfriend, a wife, a coach, or a teacher, and vice-versa for women.

■ Most women believe they may have been a man in a former life (if they believe in reincarnation).

■ Most people who are stressed will seek out the elements of religion or psychic phenomena.

■ Most people believe in some sort of ESP or telepathic communication, evidenced by a friend or loved one trying to make contact from beyond death, or even a living friend phoning just after they knew the person was about to call, before the telephone had even rung.

ACKNOWLEDGMENTS

I would like to say a very special thank-you to Mitchell Winthrop, Mark Sansonette, Susan Winthrop, Ian Leslie, Kim Lionetti, Dorian Winthrop, Paul Fegen (the Fantastic Fig), Dr. Frank "the Wizard" Milgrim, and Brian Kramer. Extra special thanks to Dr. W at The Lab and all my clients over the years who have witnessed the awesome magnetic power of mentalism and magic and have been part of an amazing experience!

INDEX